ENDING OUR

From Dissociation to Acceptance of *A Course in Miracles*

THE PRACTICE OF *A COURSE IN MIRACLES*

ENDING OUR ESCAPE FROM LOVE

From Dissociation to Acceptance of *A Course in Miracles*

KENNETH WAPNICK, PH.D.

Foundation for A COURSE IN MIRACLES®

Foundation for A COURSE IN MIRACLES®
41397 Buecking Drive
Temecula, CA 92590
www.facim.org

First printing, 2011

Printed in the United States of America

Library of Congress Cataloging-in-Publication Data

Wapnick, Kenneth, 1942-
    Ending our escape from love : from dissociation to acceptance of
    A Course in Miracles / Kenneth Wapnick.
        p. cm. -- (The practice of A Course in Miracles)
    Includes bibliographical references and index.
    ISBN 978-1-59142-513-7
    1. Course in Miracles. I. Title.
BP605.C68W3532 2011
    299'.93--dc22
                                        2011005620

CONTENTS

Preface

This current book in our series "The Practice of *A Course in Miracles*" is based on our audio publication *Escape from Love: Dissociating A COURSE IN MIRACLES*, which consists of an edited excerpt from the 2004 class "The Face of Innocence." For this book, I have expanded the central theme of dissociation to include relevant discussions from two other classes I gave in 2004, which have not been published: "Forgiveness: The End of Dissociation" and "*A Course in Miracles*: Salvation or Slavation?" (An audio excerpt of the last title has been published as "Looking with Jesus.")

The theme of resistance to *A Course in Miracles* runs through these excerpts as a thread, and it has been prominent in my teachings over the years. Indeed, it goes to the very heart of students' difficulties with the Course, as this resistance is the source of what appear to be the failures of even its most faithful adherents to learn, let alone practice, the principles of forgiveness and release of judgment. Since this problem is so very prevalent and can be the source of feelings of failure, guilt, and despair over learning how to forgive, it seemed as if it would be helpful to take these excerpts and bring them together into a unified presentation.

Ending Our Escape from Love can be seen as a companion to my earlier book *Ending Our Resistance to Love*, which also discusses the problem of resistance. I hope that these reminders will inspire students not to lose sight of their goal, even as their fear leads them to defend against it. The gentle path to Atonement begins with recognizing the fear of it, not to mention the love beyond it, and then proceeds with looking without judgment at the defenses (resistance) against our choosing to return home. Thus do the walls of dissociation dissolve and *A Course in Miracles* allowed to be the means for our accepting the Correction that heralds our awakening from the ego's dream of separation and attaining the End we seek.

These excerpts have been edited to improve their readability and make a seamless fit. The questions that served as a springboard for the discussions of dissociation have not only been edited, but often omitted to permit an easier flow of the material. As is our custom in this series, the writing has been only gently edited to reflect the informality of the actual classes.

The Appendix includes "The Secret Wall," an article in the June 2004 edition of the Foundation newsletter, *The Lighthouse*, which is relevant to the book's theme. It is largely based on excerpts from an Academy class held at the Foundation called "Forgiveness vs. Forgiveness-to-Destroy." We have also included in the Appendix Helen's poem "Stranger on the Road," which is discussed in the book.

Acknowledgments

Our Director of Publications, Rosemarie LoSasso, carefully preserved the excerpts on which this book is based, and then remarkably pulled them together into a unified whole. This was in addition to her, as always, caring and faithful preparation of the manuscript as it went through its various stages. My gratitude to her is as constant and heartfelt as has been her faithfulness to *A Course in Miracles* and our Foundation's work.

My wife Gloria provided her usual wonderful editorial advice and assistance, without which the book would not have achieved its final form. As I have written before, these "little books" were her inspiration, and each new publication renews my undying gratitude for her help, not only with these books, but for her consistent love and support for my work over almost thirty years, making it all possible. Love is indeed the way I walk in gratitude for such a sublimely noble woman.

1. The Process of Dissociation

Introduction

It is important when we work with *A Course in Miracles* over a period of many years to realize that there is a part of us that is split off, or to use the psychological term, *dissociated*. On the one hand, we have heard and read the words of the Course over and over, and the thought system makes more and more sense as the months and years of study and practice pass by. Yet, something very peculiar happens. It is almost as if a wall has been erected inside us so that there has been no carryover or direct experiential meaning in our personal lives of what we have learned and understood. In other words, we blithely go on living our lives angry and critical, indulging our specialness, getting sick and running to the doctor, and generally doing everything that normal people do—as if nothing we have studied, learned, and sworn by in this course has had an effect. It is as if there is a part of us that believes in truth, and a completely different part that lives our everyday lives as bodies dealing with all the issues our bodies are confronted with. The two parts seem totally unconnected.

1. THE PROCESS OF DISSOCIATION

It is very important as students of this course that we look at this honestly. So many of us who have been with this thought system for a long time will utter a complaint along the lines of, "When am I going to get it! When is everyone else going to get it!" What is being reflected in that is this strange dissociation that we all practice—as if, so to speak, the right hand does not know what the left hand is doing, or the right brain does not know what the left brain is doing, or the right mind does not know what the wrong mind is doing. However it is described, there is a serious split, and looking at this split or this wall is a way of understanding what Jesus means when he asks us to be honest with him and to hold nothing back (T-4.III.8:2). It makes perfect sense that we would have a wall, because this material is extremely threatening. This gets said over and over, but it appears as if we do not let it get through to us. At some point we have to address that in ourselves. We must look at it, not just intellectually, but we must try to feel what it is we do that keeps what we know to be true from permeating our lives.

This is not to say that we are not more forgiving or less judgmental than we were at the beginning of our work with this course, rather that there is a barrier.

Again, it is understandable that there would be a barrier, but simply understanding why is not enough, because that then can become a defense, and usually does. You can understand until you are blue in the face, and nothing is going to change. It is most important to try to feel what stops you from taking words you have heard and read over and over in the Course, and letting the principles affect everything in your life, because they *should* affect and change everything in your life.

It is so easy to complain about things, starting with the people with whom we live, work, or grew up, not to mention our bodies, old age, the president, the weather—everything and anything. We do that without even thinking about what we are doing. It is so natural for us to complain, find fault, separate, or exclude that we do not give it a second thought. That is one segment of our lives. Then we turn back, come to a class, study *A Course in Miracles*, do whatever we do with it, and understand it. Again, there is a gulf or wall that separates these two aspects of our experience: we understand and accept what we study in the Course as the truth, and then go about living our lives seemingly unaffected by it.

This is similar to the revolution in physics in the 20th century that started with Einstein. It shattered all of the Newtonian laws and helped us realize that nothing is what we think it is: the world of matter is basically an illusion; it is all thought, not solid. These astonishing findings have had almost no effect on anything. Most of the time, the new physics is not even taught in schools. Citing another example, there seems to be incontrovertible evidence that the United States military/intelligence had broken the Japanese code and therefore knew that there was to be an attack on Pearl Harbor. But it is so woven into the mythology of the United States that it was a sneak attack *that we knew nothing about*, that the idea that the United States had full knowledge of the planned attack has been kept separate. Then, too, everyone knows that the first gospel written was that of Mark, not Matthew, but people still talk about Matthew as the first gospel. Bibles are printed with Matthew as the first gospel, but Matthew was written second. There are dozens, hundreds, thousands of experiences like that. It is as if there is a truth on one side, and then there is what everyone does over on the other side, and never the twain shall meet. We just build a wall.

What all this tells us is that there is a tremendous fear of changing what we know—we do not want our worldview to be upset. Nothing changes or upsets our worldview more than *A Course in Miracles*, because it takes us one step, albeit a giant one, further than the quantum physicists. It not only says this world is an illusion, it says that the thought that makes up the world is an illusion, too. It is not only that this body as matter is an illusion, but the thought that made this body is also illusory. This leaves us as individuals absolutely nowhere, because it is saying that as an individual I am a total non-entity, a "no thing," a "no thought." Obviously, this is extremely frightening and overwhelming. But rather than deal with this conclusion, we split it off. Dissociation is a wonderful psychological defense, where we have two mutually exclusive thoughts, not wanting to let them go, and so we just split them off; we dissociate; we dis-associate one from the other.

Cognitive Dissonance

A variation of this dynamic is known in social psychology as *cognitive dissonance*, associated with the work of Leon Festinger in the 1950s and 1960s.

He coauthored the book *When Prophecy Fails*, which discusses the actual case of a group of believers who were certain the world was going to end on a rapidly approaching date, and that they would be rescued and safely transported away on a flying saucer (the information was received by their leader through automatic writing). They were firmly committed to this belief, attested to by their behavior: they left their jobs and spouses, and gave away their possessions and money. The dissonance would develop, Festinger and his associates theorized, when the prophecy failed, and then these believers would have to deal with the consequences of their disconfirmed expectations—they would have to find a way of reducing the cognitive dissonance. The leader did this by announcing that another message, also acquired through automatic writing, declared that the cataclysm had been called off, that so much light had been spread by the group that God had chosen to spare the world from destruction.

Another example of cognitive dissonance (post-dating Festinger's work) is that of Benjamin Creme, originally a teacher in the Alice Bailey movement (Alice Bailey was a woman who took down an extended body of spiritual information from a dis-carnate master named Djwhal Khul). Creme broke

6

with that system, and believed that a figure called the Maitreya Christ, a template of the great avatar or master (Jesus was an example of the Maitreya), was going to come back to earth and speak to the United Nations with a message of peace. He would speak in such a way that all the peoples of the world, from all languages and cultures, would understand him. Creme took out very expensive full-page ads in the New York Times, Los Angeles Times, Chicago Tribune, and other major newspapers announcing this expected appearance on a specific date.

Creme's life's work at this point rested on the belief that the Maitreya Christ would come. He said that the Maitreya had already come and was in a Middle East community in London—unknown, but he was going to announce himself. The day came and there was no announcement! In the face of this he had two choices: 1) He could admit he was wrong, but that would call his whole life into question, or 2) he could say someone made a mistake. Creme took the second option, claiming the mistaken group was the media, that the media were not ready. Therefore, even though the Maitreya Christ was here, and alive and well, he could not appear because the media and the world were not ready.

That is an example of how to reduce cognitive dissonance. You somehow have to change the external reality since you are not going to change *your* reality. That is what we all do with *A Course in Miracles*, which presents us with a tremendous problem of cognitive dissonance. On the one hand, we have our individual self: a body, a personality, a history that is so real to us, so present to us. And even though we recognize—otherwise we would not be devoting ourselves to this material—that there is something really wrong with how we are living, when we choose to participate in this *other way* that the Course represents, we resist it. Therein lies the dissonance.

Again, we have one of two choices: to change our personal reality or self, and then join in with the facts as we have them in the Course, or change the Course itself. We can change *A Course in Miracles* in many different ways: we can simply say this is not what the words mean, they mean something else, so we change the message; or we can say that there are some parts of the Course that are really right on, but there are other parts that must come from Helen's ego. That is one way to reduce the dissonance so that we do not have to deal with a body of information that contradicts not just what we believe intellectually, but our

8

very existence. Alternatively, we will say yes this is the truth, but it is not for us, or it is the truth, but it is not for us now. That way we get to keep the external reality, which in this sense is the Course, and also get to keep the personal reality of our specialness. We reduce the dissonance by splitting off these two "realities." On some level, if we are to awaken from the dream, we must deal with this.

"Do not disturb me!"

Helen Schucman's poem "Stranger on the Road"[1] expresses the attempt to reduce the dissonance coming from two different perceptions. The setting of the poem is the gospel story (Luke 24:13-33) of Jesus appearing to two disciples who were walking along the road to Emmaus after his crucifixion and burial. Initially, they did not recognize him. The two characters in the poem are Jesus and Helen, with Helen doing the talking. In the poem, Helen's longest by the

---

1. *The Gifts of God*, pp. 103-105. Reprinted in the Appendix. This, one of the most powerful of Helen Schucman's poems, was the basis for the workshop (April 1993) of the same name given when the Foundation was still in Roscoe, New York. It was published as "Forgiving Jesus: 'Stranger on the Road'."

way, she meets Jesus on the road and becomes quite upset because he is supposed to be dead.

Her first response, the first part of the poem, is to contradict what she was seeing. The reality is that this person on the road *is* Jesus, which means he was not killed, which means the thought system that would have killed him, and the thought system with which he would have identified had be been killed, is wrong, which means *her* thought system, the thought system of crucifixion, sin, guilt, fear, and death is also wrong, which means the self that arose from that thought system is wrong. She thus pleads with him, "Don't do this to me!" To think of this most un-poetically, what she is telling him is, "You are destroying my thought system, because if you are not dead, everything I believe in is wrong. And I would much rather have you be dead than to accept that everything I believe in is wrong." This means that what she wants to see is the false perception she made to conceal the true perception. Thus the importance of looking honestly: we have to look at our false perception so that we can finally look through the ego's lies to the truth that is beyond it.

This wonderful poem so clearly depicts what everyone's experience is, and specifically what everyone's experience would have to be with this course:

we do not want to see what it says, and therefore we do not see what it says. The dissonance thus disappears, so we think. It is therefore extremely helpful, as a personal exercise, to identify the various ways in which we reduce the dissonance between Jesus' thought system and ours. This will help us recognize our defenses. Another helpful exercise is to think about what happens when you read words that say your eyes do not see and your brain does not think (e.g., W-pI.92.2). Those statements are very agitating because we think we are selves with eyes that can read and that actually read these words, and a brain that takes what our eyes see and interprets it. Yet the very words tell us that our eyes do not see anything and our brain does not think—that the thoughts we think we think are not our real thoughts (W-pI.45.1). This is extremely disturbing, as is the idea that "this world was over long ago" (T-28.I.1:6). That is a most disconcerting line if you think about it. If the world were over long ago, then *I* am not here. That is the kind of thing that students tend to block in themselves so they do not feel the disturbing conflict.

Helen experienced the conflict that is talked about in this poem only because she *did* see the light, and as a result, the light was agitating. Thus, if we read this course and are not agitated, it is because we are not seeing its light, its truth. The truth is literally that this world is an hallucination, an illusion, a dream, and that our true reality is back home on a level that is not part of this world at all. This cannot help being a source of agitation to us.

Agitation is not good in one sense. No right-minded person wants anyone upset, to be in a state of disquiet; but, unfortunately, we are so ensconced in our thought system that many times the only way we can be dislodged from it is to feel agitated. Thus, what is really just a gentle reminder of the truth becomes in our experience a harsh and agitating confrontation, as Helen describes in the poem. The actual presence of Jesus is only loving and gentle; there is nothing confrontational or oppositional about it. Love simply *is*. But our fear of it, which is what resistance is, makes it into the enemy. And therefore our "friends," as one of the earlier stanzas points out, become guilt, fear, anguish, death, suffering, and separation—we are strangely comfortable with them. These are our "friends"; they are not agitating. While we may find many things in the world unpleasant, painful, and distressing, they are not agitating in the sense of being a threat to who we are. The truth of *A Course in Miracles* threatens our existence, and therefore it is agitating. If you are not aware of that, then the Course is not reaching you.

To make this point again, the reason this poem is such a wonderful teaching tool, as well as being a moving poem, is that it is not just about Helen, but about all of us who allow the light in just enough to be disturbed by it. Had Helen not seen the light, Jesus would have been just another guy on the road. It was the discrepancy between what she thought she saw— which is that he was killed and his life was snuffed out—and what she thinks she is seeing now, this resplendent being of light, that was so very upsetting. So her cry is "Do not disturb me!" It is so important that we allow ourselves to be that voice of Helen that says to Jesus and this course, "Do not disturb me! I like what I have. I don't really like it, but I like that I don't like it, because it is my dream—tread lightly on my dreams; don't take them from me."

Striking a Bargain with Truth

We can see, then, how the dynamics of dissocia- tion and reducing cognitive dissonance are what allow the wrong and right minds, the ego and the Holy Spirit, to coexist. They cannot truly coexist, just as light and darkness, love and hate (or fear) cannot coexist. They can do so, however, if they are split off, with a wall erected in between so that they remain dissociated. When Jesus tells us over and over in *A Course in Miracles* to bring the illusion to the truth, or the darkness to the light, he is talking about ending dissociation. When we bring our problems to him and look at the split mind with him, the dissociation is ended (e.g., C-4.6). When we bring the darkness to the light, the darkness disappears; when we bring the illusion to the truth, the illusion disappears; when we bring the hate to the love, the hate disappears. They do not disappear, however, if we keep them split off or dissociated. By keeping them separated, we get to have our ego's cake and eat it too. We get to have our ego, indulge all our ego's specialness, and yet have the Holy Spirit as well. In other words, we get to have our ego thought system and our lives of specialness, our bodies blissfully going along as if nothing had happened in one part of us; then there is the other part that has the Course. We just keep them separate from each other.

That is where the purpose of the workbook comes in. It is meant to be a one-year training program of applying the principles of the text to our everyday lives. The purpose of all the exercises and lessons is to end the dissociation between our life and what the Course teaches. It is terrifying to bring them together, which is why we tend to make deals with Jesus. We say we will apply forgiveness to this relationship or to this problem; or we say we have a heavy relationship with a parent we have not forgiven for decades and we will really work on that, but we will not work on forgiving the person who cut us off on the freeway, or the waiter who is rude. No, we will not work on the conflicts with those "minor, insignificant" people. We will work on how upset we have been all our lives with a specific person, but it is okay if we get angry at a figure in a news program. That is how we do it. We make a compromise or a bargain with Jesus. We are always splitting off and dissociating. Working hard on a relationship helps us put on the "face of innocence" wherein we are innocent of all aggression, since someone else made us do it (T-31.V.2-3). We go to Jesus and say, "Look, I am really working on this." Yet, what we are really doing is maintaining the wall, and then throwing him a few crumbs so he will not be angry at us.

It is so important that you not try to do something about that, other than to simply look at it. Just realize how you try to keep these truths from permeating

15

every aspect of your life, which is the name of the ego's game. If you do not come to this awareness, *A Course in Miracles* will end up hurting you, because you will have the illusion of doing what it says when you are not. Twenty-one hundred years of Christianity has hurt people. It has not brought them closer to Jesus or to God, because they have only the illusion of following Jesus. Once you have the illusion of following him, you do not have to work on it anymore. All the heathens, pagans, and heretics have to work on it, but *you* do not have to because you have already decided that you are following him. That is what people do with the Course, too. They decide that they are following what it is saying, and so they do not have to worry about it anymore. All they deal with is everyone else who does not follow it or understand it as brilliantly as they think they do.

You have to reach the point where you appreciate experientially how difficult and frightening the Course's teachings are. Be aware of how you are going to want to strike a bargain with the Course, and you should not be surprised that you do. Special relationships are bargains. We exist through bargains. As infants we learn very quickly how to make a bargain by giving our parents what they want, knowing they will give us in return what we want. Infants are masters at it, and we just get better and better at it as we grow up. Parents on their part do the same thing with their children: I will give you what you want, but you have to give me what I want. Everything is a bargain. We set up a body that is very needy, but in order for it to get what it wants, it has to bargain, pay, and sacrifice. Why would we be surprised to discover that we do the same thing with this course and its author?

We want to learn to recognize how we try to strike a bargain with the truth. Without being aware that we are doing it, we will put on this "face of innocence" that we are now this wonderful student of *A Course in Miracles*, or this wonderfully spiritual person forgiving all these difficult relationships. But we are really not letting the thought system permeate *everything* in our life, because if we did, it would literally change everything. We know that we are not letting it do that because we still get angry, critical, judgmental, and annoyed; we play special love relationships against special hate relationships, form cliques, groups, and gather allies, and we still perceive good people and bad people. It all feels so natural, as natural as breathing, because it *is* breathing—the ego's breathing. Oxygen keeps the body alive. Guilt, judgment, separation, and differences keep the ego alive—that is the ego's oxygen.

Yet, what do you do with everything else that you read in *A Course in Miracles* that part of you knows is true? What do you do, for example, with the principle that nothing happens on the level of the body? Whenever you get upset or feel good about something, you are giving the body power. You can be giving some other body power over your body. Again, there is nothing sinful about that, but it should help you humbly realize that there is a part of you that really does not want to learn this course. You want to learn those parts of it that you can feel comfortable with, and those parts that you believe will satisfy Jesus, so that he will like you and not judge you. But pay attention to how terrified you are of letting him or his love in all the way, not to mention his teachings.

There is not a Course student who does not have ambivalent feelings about it and about Jesus, God, love, forgiveness, and so on. These feelings are understandable, as I have been saying. Since time is not real, the same choice that confronted us in the ontological instant confronts us all the time. This is the choice between the ego's thought system of separation, which leads to sin, guilt, fear, hate, and fear of death, and the thought system of the Holy Spirit, the thought system of the Atonement that says the separation never happened, which leads to experiences of love and peace. We all made the wrong choice together as one collective Son, and we continually make the same wrong choice until the point comes when we throw up our hands in despair and say there must be another way, at which point we open up our minds to the possibility of another way of looking.

2. Discussion

The Wall of Anger

Q: I probably am projecting my guilt onto you because I heard you being impatient with us—that we are not doing it right or fast enough.

A: What I often say, based on some passages in the Course (e.g., T-17.VI) is that you can always tell the meaning of something by noticing where you end up with it. Where you end up is the goal you had set from the start, and everything else becomes the means to get there. Thus, where you have ended up is that I am the enemy—impatient, angry, and judgmental—and you are the victim. Here you are sincerely trying to do your very best, and I come along and do this to you. You end up as the innocent victim and I the victimizer. What follows is that if I am the enemy, then you do not have to listen to me anymore. Who would want to listen to someone yelling, screaming, judging, castigating, and being unkind, unloving, and insensitive? Part of you would feel justified in concluding that you do not have to pay any attention to what I say or write.

If you do not want to go down that road, then just remind yourself that whatever you are feeling *is* the outcome you desired; otherwise you would not feel it. Remember, this is your dream. Therefore, if you are feeling angry, unheard, or judged, which then leads you to conclude that you are not going to listen to me, that is the outcome you wanted. At that point, a legitimate question to ask yourself is why you would want that. Pursuing that would lead you to a very fruitful point in your process.

The purpose of my speaking about dissociation is to help students look at the fact that there is a wall; otherwise they cannot get past it. Then the challenge, the hard part, is to look at this without judgment. Putting up the wall is a reflection of the original wall that we put up, and none of us is in touch with that. Discovering the wall of dissociation helps us get in touch with the same content of the ontological wall. The guilt over that "original sin" is enormous, and then guilt stops it cold, preventing any undoing since guilt is a wall. You cannot deal with a problem that you do not recognize.

The first step, thus, is simply to recognize the feelings you have in response to being told about the split, the dissociation. One outcome, as we have seen, is to be angry with me and then to erect a wall between us. Another is to feel guilty or very sad about it. That then ends up as a wall, too—not necessarily a wall between you and me, but in the sense that the fear becomes so intolerable and painful that it stops you: "I am a terrible person—look what I am doing!" That is just as effective a defense as anger. The challenge is to be able to look at all of that, whether in the form of anger, guilt, sorrow, sadness, or anything else, and move past it. The way you move past it is to just recognize it and look at it. We will be stressing this point throughout the discussion.

The Wall of Resistance

Q: Last year I was in a bad place. I was at the wall, I think. I realized that I do not want to do what Jesus says. I was feeling hopeless and scared. I read Lesson 74 with your commentary,[2] and I went over the wall, and I just now realized that the wall for me was the original belief in sin. In doing the lesson, I started to give Jesus my feelings of hopelessness and victimization.

---

2. *Journey through the Workbook of "A Course in Miracles"*- Vol. Two.

Then my ego got really smart and lay down for about a month. So now I have forgiven myself. Getting past the wall has had an amazingly powerful effect on every aspect of my life.

A: What helps us get past that wall more and more is to realize how good it feels when we do what Jesus says, and how terrible it feels to have that wall up and to play a game with Jesus: "I am not going to do the lesson the way you say; I am not going to do this, I am not going to do that!" We need to feel the pain of that infantile brattiness, and how good it feels when we finally let that go. It is very simple, but that is the problem—that it is simple. The ego loves complexity. You may recall the concept of Occam's Razor from your college days, the principle, *simply stated*, that simple explanations of phenomena are preferable to complex ones.[3]

The worst thing you can do is to resist the resistance or to devise techniques to get past it. Techniques might work, and people are very skillful at that kind of thing these days, but the techniques do not undo the resistance. In Freud's early work, he was very attracted to hypnosis, as many people were in the 1880s and

---

3. William of Occam (1290-1349).

1890s. Freud studied under the noted neurologist Jean-Marie Charcot, who was an early champion of hypnosis, and while Freud felt that hypnotism could uncover some unconscious material, he later became rather critical of it. He concluded in his findings that hypnosis did nothing with the resistance—for the most part, in effect, it merely did an end run around it, circumventing the process of true healing.

The idea is not to do anything with the resistance. Don't hypnotize it away or utilize techniques to break it down. Instead, acknowledge that the resistance is there, and allow yourself to feel its effects. The resistance is the wall. William Thetford had a cute saying: "If it's not in the workbook, don't do it." There is nothing in the workbook about hypnosis or other techniques. All that it teaches is that we should look at the ego without judgment, recognizing the cost to us of identifying with it. In one way or another, that is what *A Course is Miracles* is about—looking at the ego and at our resistance, and asking Jesus or the Holy Spirit to help us look without judgment.

Yet, we all want to do something more than that. I spoke about this tendency at length in my recent workshop on the section in the text called "I Need Do Nothing" (T-18.VII). The body is the ego's doing something about itself, to preserve the illusion that there really is an ego, the separated self. The body does not and cannot do anything because it is merely the puppet, animated by the mind, the puppeteer. As Jesus says in the text:

> Can you paint rosy lips upon a skeleton, dress it in loveliness, pet it and pamper it, and make it live? And can you be content with an illusion that you are living? (T-23.II.18:8-9).

Therefore, the focus should never be on the lifeless piece of wood (the *skeleton*), but on the "brains" behind it. The body indeed appears to do something, for it was established to solve a problem that does not exist. Our physical self, along with the world that is its home are, as I like to put it, *maladaptive solutions to a nonexistent problem*. In this sense we can understand that the mind, too, does not do anything, for that would mean that there were something that needed to be done, that the ego needed to be undone. Yet all that needs to be undone is the mind's *belief* that there is an ego that is the problem that needs to be solved. So, again, the mind, believing it is an ego (a *something*), makes up a world and body that is also a *something*. And thus we are diverted from ever recognizing the true problem: the decision maker that believes the lie of separation, and then believes the stories of the world and body that support the lie and reinforce the insane belief that it is true.

Again, the problem is not the resistance or the wall. The problem is that we *want* the wall, and it is a problem because there *is* no wall. Resistance is not an entity or a thing. It is the end product of our *wanting*, the result of the fear of the love that the resistance hides. We live in a society that wants everything to be done fast. We want instant everything—from instant food, sexual pleasure, and money, to instant solutions to problems. That works perfectly for the ego's purposes because, again, these are all ways of solving the problem of our various appetites, and that problem does not exist. Moreover, the real appetite, which is for guilt as the preservative of our individual self, does not exist either.

Again, what we need to do with the resistance is nothing but be aware of it, which means be aware of the thought that says, "I am too afraid of the truth, so I want to split it off." We want to split the truth off from illusion, because if we bring the two together, we will disappear as we know ourselves to be as special individuals. Jesus is teaching us to be aware that there is a wall, and that the effects of that wall do not feel good. Indeed, we want *not* to feel good; we want the end product that is the seeming reality of our separated self. We need to be willing to say that that is where we are, and that it is okay. *Do not try to fix yourself,* Jesus tells us, for that need to fix ourselves is the problem. *A Course in Miracles* is not a fixer. That is why so many people drop it not long after their initial attraction to it—and for good reason, because this is not really what they want. They want a quick fix. They want instant spirituality. Just as people want an instant drug high, people want an instant "God high." This course does not give it. This course is a lot of hard work. It is a lot of hard work in learning not to do anything—that is hard. Paradoxically, hard work is easy because it reinforces the lie about ourselves, supporting the belief that there is a problem that needs hard fixing. People may think that they are lazy, that they do not want to work, but laziness is part of the hard/easy work of preserving and perpetuating the lie of separation and specialness.

The "hard" work comes in learning that you need do nothing about the resistance. What you want to do, once again, is simply be aware. Do whatever magic is going to get you through the day and through the pain—emotional or physical. It is fine to work on the symptom. After all, no one wants to be in pain, and so if there is a quick way of getting rid of the pain, by all means use it. Just do not delude yourself into thinking that that is getting rid of the *source* of the pain. It will get rid of the symptom, and it is cruel to withhold something that will alleviate a symptom just because it is not "spiritual." However, if you really want to help others with the *cause* of their pain, the underlying source, you do not *need* to do anything. Just love them, be kind, and accept them. On the one hand, you may help them with the symptom, which can be very loving. On the other hand, do not *do* anything about the cause, because when you do something about the cause, you are making it real. When you do something about the resistance, you are making the resistance real. This is exactly what your ego wants. *Do not fight against it.* Again, just be aware that there is a wall and say, "This is what I am doing"; but at the same time, try to allow yourself as best you can to experience the effects of the wall. That's all. Don't do anything else.

Most of us realize that at times we are keeping ourselves from dealing with an issue—something external upsets us, say, and then we realize we do not want to deal with the underlying issue and so we block it out. Later we feel that we have to do something about that block. But even in these cases we need to learn to do nothing. The problem is our resistance, not the underlying issue we think is there. For example, if my supervisor changes my schedule at work without discussing it with me, I feel hurt and not respected, not recognizing that what happened would not have bothered me, however justified the world would have seen my being upset, if I had not first rejected love, not respecting *it*. We need always to return to the mind's decision to reject love as the cause of *everything* that upsets or concerns us. The problem is not what we think it is, to which we are resistant, but rather our decision-making mind's choosing the wrong teacher, *and our resistance to returning to the mind and choosing again—against the ego and for the Holy Spirit.*

Resistance says there is an underlying problem that I do not want to look at. But the fact of the matter is that there *is* no underlying problem. Freud said that analysis of resistance is the central issue in psychoanalysis. This underlying resistance says there is a serious problem that I do not want to look at—my sin and guilt—and it is so horrendous I do not want ever to look at it. Resistance then becomes the defense. When I am able to let go of the resistance, which is what looking with Jesus or the Holy Spirit means, then I suddenly realize that there was nothing there. As the Course says:

> What if you looked within and saw no sin? (T-21.IV.3:1).

This idea, the core of the Atonement, reflects the deeper truth that the *tiny, mad idea* of being separate from our Creator (T-27.VIII.6:2) is nothing either. That is, there really is no *tiny, mad idea*. The thought system of the entire world is a defense against recognizing the nothingness of this insane thought. That is why we are really angry at the Holy Spirit or Jesus— They do not even deal with the *tiny, mad idea*; the ego does. We have to believe there is a *tiny, mad idea* because that is who we are. The Holy Spirit's response, however, is, "What tiny, mad idea?" The acceptance of the Atonement is the acceptance of the truth that nothing happened to separate our Self from perfect Oneness and Love.

Thus, resistance is ultimately related to recognizing the inherent nothingness of the separated self, as we read in the text:

> The ego is nothing more than a part of your belief about yourself. Your other life [our life as

spirit, our true Self] has continued without inter-
ruption, and has been and always will be totally
unaffected by your attempts to dissociate it
(T-4.VI.1:6-7).

We know *A Course in Miracles* teaches this, and we
understand the words, but we keep this principle split
off and live our lives as if it were not true. The fear of
this inherent nothingness of our special self can be
experienced as a sense of loss, and to deal with it we
sometimes go so far as to resurrect old problems or
issues that have already been dealt with. In the strange
and perverse way that is the ego, our problems and
grievances are a source of comfort when we are feeling threatened to the core by suddenly comprehend-
ing what the Course is saying.

Remember, the ego is not a thing; the ego is really
us. We inevitably feel a sense of loss of self when we
begin to forgive more and look at the body differently.
That is when our resistance escalates and, as Jesus
explains in the text, suspiciousness turns to vicious-
ness (T-9.VII.4:7). Sickness is one way of defending
against the truth that frightens us (see W-pI.136). We
tend to get scared when the light of the truth of Who
we are begins to break through the darkness of our
mind, and all of a sudden we recognize what that

means: namely, that the light will shine on this self and dissolve it, because there is no self here in the world where we think we exist. This self, this body, continues to exist because our wrong-minded self chooses not to see it. Thus the body remains in the darkness of guilt and so we cannot see it for what it really is. Guilt's darkness enshrouds it and so we think there is something here, but in truth there is nothing here, and if we shine the light of Atonement on it, there *will* be nothing there in our experience.

The wall is our resistance to looking at nothing, realizing it is nothing. Being an individual, a body, is intrinsically bound up with attack. There is a passage from "The Little Hindrance" in Chapter 26 that I quote frequently in this regard:

> Each day, and every minute in each day, and every instant that each minute holds, you but re-live the single instant when the time of terror took the place of love (T-26.V.13:1).

At every single instant we are reliving that original moment when we believed we destroyed God and experienced the ensuing terror born of our perception of His retaliative wrath. Everything is a reliving of that moment because time is not linear. We just relive that original instant over and over in different forms.

It is a kaleidoscope of guilt, for each time we "turn" it—the multitudinous projections into form—we get different shapes. There may be colored pieces of glass that are pretty (special love), but it is always the same guilt. No matter how we turn the kaleidoscope, it is still the same guilt.

Everything is an attack. Being born is an attack. What we want to do in the early steps of the process is to stop trying to pretend that we are kind, loving, nice, sweet, thoughtful, and spiritual persons. As I like to say, those kinds of people stay in Heaven; they do not come here. "Bad guys" come here. The problem is that not only are we the bad guys, but that without anger and judgment we will cease to exist. That is why the practice of this course is so hard: anger is the foundation of the wall and therefore of our special self. That is why we maintain the dissociation. We do not want to expose the illusion to the truth. We do not wish to bring the nothingness to the Everything, because when we do, the nothingness is gone. It is not that we are afraid of the Everything, because we do not know what the Everything is. We are afraid of not being *nothing*. When we look at nothingness with the Love of the Everything beside us, it dissolves. That is the fear. That is why we keep erecting a barrier. And that is what we really have to look at.

To repeat this very important point: Resistance to this course arises from our fear that if we practice it as it was meant to be practiced, we are going to lose. Underlying that, however, is the fear that in practicing this we are going to win everything; but then that means we lose our self. The point I have been making is that it is really important to look at the fear—the real fear and its effects, and how we try to keep the Course at arm's length.

The Decision Maker as Victimizer

Q: After I got involved in the Course, I began to feel victimized by the decision maker, that I was "forced" into situations that I consciously did not want, such as medical conditions, for example.

A: This is another expression of dissociation. You are splitting off the decision maker from yourself, which is what the ego wants you to do, because the decision maker is the only thing there is. We are always the decision maker. Once we chose to leave Heaven, or believed we could leave, we became a decision maker. In Heaven, there is only the one Son, Christ. But once we believed we separated, our Identity as Christ became a rapidly fading memory. The post-separation self is *always* the decision maker. That self-concept never changes. We try to hide it and make up stories about ourselves that we are not a decision-making self, but a guilty, sinful self. This is established by the fact that we are mindless bodies, and without a mind, *the only decision-making agent*, how can we be responsible for our condition or situation? And so, being bodies, we are innocent, and everyone and everything else is responsible for us, and therefore guilty. The bottom line, however, is that since *ideas leave not their source*, we never stopped being a decision maker. Jesus' *only* purpose in this course is to undo the dissociation that seems to split ourselves off from our decision-making self.

Thus, the process of *looking* at yourself or a loved one suffering from cancer, for example, is what begins to end that dissociation. The *you* that is looking is the observing self, the decision maker. When the decision maker chooses to be in its right mind, it becomes an observer. The observing self is looking at someone having cancer and dying, or looking at someone doing anything at all. What that helps us do

36

is end the identification with the ego self, the bodily self, and begin to re-identify with what we have always been: the decision maker. We need to be aware that feeling victimized by the decision maker is no different than being victimized by your parents or anyone else.

Whatever is happening is what we as decision-making minds want, despite how we are pretending to feel. We would all agree that pain is something we do not want, but if we were to look at what is going on in our minds, we would realize that we in fact luxuriate in the pain. I have occasionally told this story about a patient I was seeing many years ago. He had a love affair end and was in a great deal of pain over the breakup. He would not let go of the pain, but his self-indulgence in this regard ended when he one day admitted to me that he actually found the pain to be exquisite, a lovely word for what he was feeling. Actually, all pain is exquisite, and it is this we have to look at, and that is most difficult. We read near the end of the text:

> If you can be hurt by anything, you see a picture of your secret wishes. Nothing more than this. And in your suffering of any kind you see your own concealed desire to kill (T-31.V.15: 8-10).

2. DISCUSSION

This is what Jesus means by "the secret of salvation":

> The secret of salvation is but this: that you are doing this unto yourself (T-27.VIII.10:1).

Accepting this fact of salvation is what ends the face-of-innocence dynamic, wherein we willingly and happily choose to suffer so that we may point an accusing finger at our assailant, saying with great glee:

> "Behold me, brother, at your hand I die" (T-27.I.4:6).

My doing this to myself means there is no external cause. I am both the cause and the effect, and since the effect is terrible, I want to change the cause. I want to change from a decision-making self that chose the ego, to a decision-making self that chooses the Holy Spirit. Then I can look at the nothingness and realize it is nothing. The so-called reality of the world rests on the ego's dynamic of convincing us that we should not look at the nothingness because it is really something, something dreadful. But the world lies. And so, as Jesus asks us in the text, referring to the ego as a stranger who wandered into our home:

> Ask not this transient stranger, "What am I?" He

is the only thing in all the universe that does not know. Yet it is he you ask, and it is to his answer that you would adjust. This one wild thought, fierce in its arrogance, and yet so tiny and so meaningless it slips unnoticed through the universe of truth, becomes your guide. To it you turn to ask the meaning of the universe. And of the one blind thing in all the seeing universe of truth you ask, "How shall I look upon the Son of God?" (T-20.III.7:5-10).

This, of course, makes no sense, especially with the Voice of wisdom and truth available to us, awaiting our decision.

3. The Personal Self versus the Impersonal Self

Summarizing what we have said about the wall so far, we can say that the wall itself is a symbol of the process of dissociation. We believe what *A Course in Miracles* says is true, and then there is our everyday life. The wall represents the fact that we have split one off from the other, so that the two can never be brought together. Life in the body is inherently meaningless—whether we are talking about our personal body, the bodies of loved ones, bodies in the world, or the world itself. The only meaning life here has is learning that life is meaningless. As Jesus says early on in the text:

> How else can you find joy in a joyless place except by realizing that you are not there? (T-6.II.6:1).

Without learning this lesson, we will not be ready to take the next step, which is knowing that life's only meaning is helping us get from what we think our lives are to what our lives truly are. This is our only true joy.

The problem is that we do not think our lives here are meaningless. That is the dissociation. In one part of our minds we understand, believe, and accept as true what the Course says, which is that life here is meaningless, and that "There is no life outside of Heaven" (T-23.II.19.1). Then in the other part of our minds, we believe our lives to be meaningful, as seen by our reactions to ourselves, loved ones, and events and situations in the world. In a sense, everyone's wall is the same—even though the forms differ—because dissociation is dissociation. Whether we feel our lives are wonderful, meaningful, and joyful, or meaningless, painful, and a failure, we are still making life real. Pleasure and pain are the same in this sense, reinforcing our belief that the body is real (see, e.g., T-19.IV-A.17:10-11; T-19.IV-B.12). That is one side, which we keep separated from the truth that our lives are not pleasurable or painful, meaningful or meaningless, for what is nonexistent can have no feeling or meaning.

As I said earlier, if this discussion evokes anger in you, it is because of the underlying guilt over splitting God off, in essence saying that you do not care about Him or about Jesus and his course—all you care about is your life, which you have judged to be meaningful. The anger, thus, is really about getting caught again, so to speak, with your hand in the cookie jar, in telling truth to get lost. That is where the guilt is lodged, and guilt demands punishment, which means you believe you deserve to be judged and scolded because you got caught.

I will tell you a cute true story about getting caught. Many years ago I did a workshop in Colorado outside Aspen, and while there I gave a talk at a nearby Trappist monastery. The former abbot of that monastery, who was deeply loved and respected by the community, had an affair and impregnated the sister of one of the monks, necessitating his leaving the monastery and getting married. The couple attended the workshop, and at one point when I was talking about special relationships, I noticed that he had his arm around her, and I, being the pain in the neck that I am, pointed to them and jokingly said, "We'll have none of that here!" And in response the former monk said: "There I go again. I'm always getting caught!" And that is where our anger ultimately comes from: the guilt over getting caught—again!

Still one more time, we all want to keep *A Course in Miracles* separate from our personal lives, because we believe our personal life *is* our life. We actually believe we have a personal life, and that belief is the problem. *There is no personal life in Heaven.* That is another way of understanding why we left Heaven—God does not recognize personal existence. There was a lovely book written some time in the early part of the 20th century called *The Impersonal Life*, a channeled book by an unknown author. This is the impersonal life that we do not want, which is why we made ourselves into a person, a body, and a personality. The truth is that we desperately want to keep the truth of our *im*personal life split off by the wall of dissociation. We make the wall out of concrete and steel, and then fortify it so we will not get hurt. To make it appear as if that is not what we are doing, we make a little hole or crack in the concrete so that a little bit of love can appear to come through. And so we tell Jesus, "Yes, I am forgiving and I am learning what you are telling me." Yet *I* am the one who is doing it, practicing forgiveness, but on my own terms.

When I speak of the fourth of the six stages in the development of trust (M-4.I-A), I emphasize that its state of peace, following the first three stages that entail letting go of our belief in sacrifice, is forgiveness. We have learned that we feel better when we let go of judgment. Yet Jesus' response to our feeling that we have "made it," having worked through some rather difficult relationships and situations, is to say to us:

> He [the teacher of God] has not yet come as far
> as he thinks (M-4.I.6:10).

This ushers in the fifth stage, the Course's version of the "dark night of the soul," the term St. John of the Cross used to describe this stage that precedes our enlightenment. It is usually experienced as hell because we suddenly recognize that the fourth stage was not the end, for there was still a sense of *I*, the person that was forgiving. Our personal life was retained, the *I* that was doing the forgiving.

In the sixth stage, the real world, there is no *I*. However, we cannot get from the fourth to the sixth without going through the fifth, and that may take a very long time, Jesus says, because in this stage we recognize that the self we thought we were is not a self. Not only is it not *our* self, it is *no* self. In order to avoid having that happen, we build a wall of dissociation.

Once again, what students do with *A Course in Miracles* is a wonderful example of this dynamic of dissociation, resulting in two mutually exclusive contradictory thought systems seeming to coexist. The only way that can happen, as I said earlier, is to split them off so they both continue to exist in separate parts of the mind. There are walls and locked doors— the same house, but one cannot get from one part to the other. This is reminiscent of the original dissociation when we split off from God. We said, in effect, "I want a personal life, which I will now render meaningful as my life of specialness. My true life as an impersonal Son of God, part of the living and loving Oneness of God, will be split off from me. I may let little memories come up from time to time, little feelings of love, union, and joining will come through, but for the most part I will keep it all separate." This need and desire to perpetuate our personal self cannot exist without the price of tremendous guilt.

That is what we all are doing and we need to look at it. We are not going to make the progress we want to make in this course if we do not look at the mind's *decision* to be an ego, because that decision is the problem. The guilt over the dissociation is enormous, as I have been emphasizing. Guilt keeps it going, because the guilt drives the problem even further underground. Recall the trenchant line in the text that says the problem is not *what* we dissociate, but the fact *that* we dissociate. Note that this comes in the context of Jesus teaching us that dissociation is a decision to forget, which then causes us to become fearful:

Unless you first know something you cannot dissociate it. Knowledge must precede dissociation, so that dissociation is nothing more than a decision to forget. What has been forgotten then appears to be fearful, but only because the dissociation is an attack on truth. You are fearful *because* you have forgotten. And you have replaced your knowledge by an awareness of dreams because you are afraid of your dissociation, not of what you have dissociated. When what you have dissociated is accepted, it ceases to be fearful (T-10.II.1).

Freud's mistake was in thinking the problem was *what* a person dissociates—that there is something rotten there that must be looked at. He failed to recognize that there is nothing rotten. In contrast to Freud, Jesus says, to repeat this central point, that the problem is not *what* we dissociate but *that* we dissociate. In other words, it does not matter what we split off and what we do not want to look at. The problem is simply that we are splitting off, that we are actively choosing to be separate. This is where the guilt is, because it is reminiscent, as is everything in the world, of the original splitting off from our Source. Similarly, defenses are not the problem; it is the idea that we think we need defenses that is the problem. It makes no sense, after all, to defend against a problem that is not there.

What makes *A Course in Miracles* so impressive as a spiritual path, and as a *practical* spiritual path, is that Jesus clearly defines its metaphysical basis—everything comes from the original *tiny, mad idea* that we took seriously—and then teaches us that our lives are merely a reliving over and over and over again of that original *tiny, mad idea* taken seriously. Everything we do here is a fragmentary shadow, not of a distant past, but of a decision-making present. This is another crucial aspect of the Course's metaphysics—that linear time is an illusion and everything is being chosen and therefore is occurring right now. In this sense, the structure of the mind is not horizontal; past, present, and future are vertical. Time goes up and down basically, which means that what we experience at the top of the iceberg—our conscious experience—is a horrifying fragment that is continually being generated from this ever-present, more horrifying guilt. Re-quoting this important passage:

> Each day, and every minute in each day, and every instant that each minute holds, you but relive the single instant when the time of terror took the place of love (T-26.V.13:1).

We need not go back to that original instant, for what seemed to have happened *then* is happening *now*, and thus need only be dealt with now. If I am angry, it is because I am guilty; and if I am guilty, it is because I am dissociating God and substituting the love of myself for His Love. That is the bottom line. Specialness is always substitution. In Chapter 18, the first section called "The Substitute Reality" equates substitution and specialness (T-18.I): in specialness we substitute our love for another for our love for God. That is why there is so much guilt associated with specialness.

Our special love for another person masks our special love for God, but that in turn masks our true love for our Creator, which the "Fear of Redemption" section I cited earlier discusses (T-13.III). Each time we are attracted to someone or something in this world, we are being motivated by an underlying need for salvation, which is at the core of all specialness and addictions. It does not matter whether it is a special love relationship with a person, pet, food, drug, or alcohol. Whatever the form, our craving a special object for our love is saying: God's Love and peace are not enough for me; the peace I get from a fifth of scotch or bottle of wine, a shot of heroin, or being with a nice warm body makes me feel loved and appreciated, thus removing the terrible feeling of aloneness.

It cannot be said often enough that there must be guilt in specialness because it is reminiscent of the original moment, which is ongoing, in which we, in effect, say to God: "Get lost; I do not need you. If you will not give me the love that I want, I will find it elsewhere." Thus, we made up a world of substances, things, causes, and groups; we made up everything so that we could find in the world the love He would not give us. Our devotion to this goal leads to enormous guilt.

The major reason people have so much trouble with *A Course in Miracles*, and particularly with special relationships and all the sections on it, is that Jesus is catching us with our hands in the proverbial cookie jar. He is saying, "I have your number." He is not saying it in anger or in judgment, but he *is* saying, "I want you to look at what you are doing." This is so important because you cannot change what you are doing if you do not know that you are doing it. It is so easy to make compromises with spirituality and not know you are making them. The ego is so slippery. Specialness is quite insidious; and special love is the most insidious defense of all. It seems to be so holy, wonderful, and sweet; it makes you feel so good. If it is *spiritual* specialness (such as: "I am a student of *A Course in Miracles* and you aren't!"), all the better; it makes you feel so holy. All your specialness needs are being met, but it is being done in the name of God, making it even more impervious to correction, until you look at it and see how you have split off and dissociated the truth of the Course.

At the end of Lesson 358 we read:

> *Let me not forget myself is nothing, but my Self is all* (W-pII.358.1:7).

We split off the fact that our self is nothing, which means that our Self is all. We split that off from our conscious experience, which is that our self is everything. It does not matter whether this self is wonderful, glorious, joyful, important, spiritual, holy, or it is the dregs of the earth—miserable, an abject failure, incompetent, incapable, despicable. It does not matter. Wonderful or terrible, we nonetheless believe we have a self, and therefore we must split that off from the Course's truth that says, "Let me not forget myself is nothing, but my Self is all." The guilt over that is what continually drives us not to look, because guilt is the threat that if we look at this, we will see that our sin is so horrific and awful that God cannot but punish us. The terror of this escalates to the point that we just block the whole thing from awareness and continue to dissociate. Guilt (or better: the *decision* for guilt) is therefore the problem, because it is the guilt that warns us not to look within. Instead, as minds we make up a world in which we continually express our guilt through projection, but this is not our fault since the other's sin struck us first. In the end, the ego has us believe that our face is truly the "face of innocence."

4. The Wall Dissolves

Q: I had this dream last night that I was in a place that I called my home, but it really wasn't my home. There was a big mountain behind it, and then I have a retaining wall, which is very long to keep the rats from falling onto our property. In the middle of it there was a huge dragon that when I saw it I thought, "My god, I better get this thing out of here dead or alive!" The whole wall is about to fall on us and just destroy our house. What to do? I woke up petrified and started to cry, just as I had after you talked about dissociation yesterday. At the time, I did not realize the connection with the wall you have been talking about—it just hit me now.

A: I assume full responsibility for your dream! That is an interesting dream and is self-explanatory. The ego says that if you take the wall down you will be devoured by the dragon, when all that will really happen is that you will disappear into the Heart of God. To the part of us that likes being who we are as individuals, the Heart of God is this fire-breathing dragon that will devour us. There are other parts to the dream that are important, but I think that is the gist of it. The basic fear is, "Where would I be without my wall?"

Interestingly, you were not crying in the dream, but only after you woke up. What that crying reflects is the guilt over the fact that you are still pushing love away; you are pushing this course, Jesus, and God away. We all would have overwhelming guilt over that, so overwhelming in fact that we would not want to look at it. Therefore, it comes out in dreams, which often show us a part of ourselves we do not want to look at. I think it is important to understand that one cannot live like that—pushing love away—without guilt. Everyone walks around with guilt, including devoted students of the Course, because they are not aware they are continually pushing its teachings away.

The wall cannot be undone by trying to knock it down. What will help the most is simply looking at it and acknowledging—without judgment—that you are putting the wall up and dissociating. Remind yourself, though, that you are doing this not because you are a bad person, but because you are fearful. Moreover, not only are you fearful, you are insane, because the ego has convinced you there is a dragon on the other side. As long as we believe there is a dragon, we will feel justified in maintaining a wall because if we do not have a wall, this self we think we are will be devoured and rendered nonexistent.

That is why this process takes time. Even though linear time is an illusion, within the illusion of time this takes time because we are so fearful. This is why *A Course in Miracles* has to be read, studied, and practiced over and over again. The fear is enormous. What happens over time, however, is that we learn to develop a relationship with Jesus, the Holy Spirit, or any other symbol of the Love of God, which allows us to begin to learn not to be so afraid of looking beyond the wall. Thus, Jesus tells us in the section "The Fear to Look Within":

> Loudly the ego tells you not to look inward, for if you do your eyes will light on sin, and God will strike you blind (T-21.IV.2:3).

This is the dragon. It takes a great deal of time and trust to get to the point where you would be able to look without guilt and know that there is nothing there. Recall:

> What if you looked within and saw no sin? (T-21.IV.3:1).

4. THE WALL DISSOLVES

The first step in the process is to forgive yourself for having a wall, for dissociating and pushing God away. Remember, you cannot look without judgment until you know that that is what you are doing. If you do not think there is a problem, you are not going to seek the answer. That is why the ego is always teaching us to "seek but do not find." Of course, it does not tell us that we are not going to find what we look for, but Jesus does, explaining that we do not find it because we are looking in the wrong place: in the world, in the body, and even in this course for an answer that we will never find, because the problem is that our minds dissociate, splitting love off because we think it will hurt us. Yes, love *will* hurt our personal self, but this is true only from the perspective of the personal self. It is essential that we see the wall, to see how we dissociate, and to see it all the time.

The idea is to look without guilt and without judging, justifying, rationalizing, or denying the dissociation, but at the same time to see it clearly. That is what a relationship with the Holy Spirit or with Jesus means: looking at the ego without judgment. That is all it is. Very simple! Don't change your ego; don't come at it with an axe or a sledgehammer and try to break down the wall. Don't do anything with the wall except look at it, because it is the *not* looking at it that keeps it intact. Looking at it would allow it to dissolve, which is why Jesus tells us that the solid wall of granite we think is there ends up as a fragile veil without power to keep the light away (e.g., T-18.IX. 5-6; T-22.III.3,5).

You will be able to experience that more and more when there is no fear of the light; and there will be less and less fear of the light as there is less and less judgment. Of course, if there is less judgment, less anger, and less attack, there will be less guilt. As guilt lessens, more light is allowed in. That does not break down the wall of dissociation, it dissolves it. Remember that Jesus describes the process as "a quiet melting in" (T-18.VI.14:6). We do not attack the body. The "quiet melting in" does not mean that the body will physically melt away, but that our investment in it will. This means we would no longer see the body as something real in itself, the desired end being a continually healthy, youthful, and attractive body, for example. Rather, we will see the body as a means, and therefore it will not matter what the body does or what it is like, because it will now serve but the single purpose of being a "learning device" (T-2.IV.3:1) for the mind's learning of forgiveness. All that is important is that it become a means to an end. That is the quiet and gentle "melting in." We do not break it down or fight against it. Looking at the body quietly and gently is what allows the wall to dissolve.

Once again, you need to acknowledge that you want the wall and then recognize that splitting off the truth from your own life is causing you pain. If that does not happen, you will still want the wall and not be motivated to give it up. You have to realize that having the wall, keeping love away, not letting love, kindness, and gentleness be a part of all your relationships—the big ones and the little ones—is painful. That is the only way to find the peace we truly want, the peace this world cannot give.

Students of this course have often said that the only times they make a real effort to practice what they learn and read is when things are really terrible in their lives—only when things are really bad do they feel motivated to put *A Course in Miracles* into practice. Then, however, it feels as if they are being called on to sacrifice, and that is certainly not in keeping with the Course's principles.

Purpose is key to resolving this conflict. The Catholic Church—although it is not the Catholic Church alone that exemplifies this insane thinking—

places great value on sacrifice and suffering. Suffering and being in pain are seen as good, because they lead to a greater end, being part of God's plan of redemption. I once heard Mother Teresa give a talk to a group of nuns during which she said that "suffering is a kiss from God." That was her theology, and it worked very well for her. *A Course in Miracles*, on the other hand, says that suffering is an inevitable by-product of our resistance to God's Love. It is thus not part of God's Will at all. It is not that the Holy Spirit or Jesus wants us to suffer. It is our resistance and our fear of the truth and of love that causes the pain. If we are suffering, it is very tempting to say that we are innocent of this, and that someone or something else is doing it to us—even: "Why is Jesus letting this happen? Why is this course doing this? Everything was fine until I started reading it! Now everything is terrible. It's not fair!" Yet, all this is but another form of the "face of innocence," a quasi-spiritual "face of innocence." "Why doesn't Jesus intervene and do something!" we scream. "Why doesn't God stop the pain?"

From the Course's point of view, pain is a choice we make. Unfortunately, since we are so guilt-ridden, pain is experienced more as atonement. Therefore, as a correction, if you start to experience pain, misery, and unhappiness as anything other than your own choice, try to realize that that, too, is an attempt to maintain that you are innocent, or else that you are so terribly rotten and neurotic that you cannot think of yourself any other way. In back of that, though, is the "face of innocence," meaning someone made you this way. Your problems are not your fault.

So, yes, it is true that we do not have to suffer. That makes *A Course in Miracles* different from many other spiritualities, especially traditional Christian ones that teach that we *do* need to suffer and sacrifice—after all, the great model of Christianity is Jesus, and God knows he suffered, at least in terms of the Christian myth and Church teachings.

Our suffering comes from resistance, as I have been explaining, but we can at least look at the fact that it is *our* resistance, and so we do not have to suffer anymore. This could then motivate us to let it and the wall go. Recall the line I quoted earlier from the end of Chapter 27:

> The secret of salvation is but this: that you are doing this unto yourself (T-27.VIII.10:1).

That is very hard for our egos because it puts the responsibility for our pain and suffering squarely on us. We read that line in the Course and believe and accept what it says—at least we think we do—but then we do not live it. When something happens, we immediately look elsewhere for the cause of our distress and unhappiness. On the bodily level there are very real causes for our distress, but that is not where the ultimate cause lies. This is why no one will ever find the ultimate cause for disease, and social, economic, and political problems. Problems will always be with us until we undo *the* problem: the mind's belief in separation.

One of the key points of the workbook—underscored in the Introduction, and also in the text and manual—is *generalization*. That is the goal of any authentic teaching. Teachers want their students to learn what they are teaching, and then to generalize it. Jesus, as our teacher, wants us to learn what he is teaching about forgiveness and to generalize it to all relationships. The beginning of the teacher's manual (M-3) talks about three levels of relationships. The first level comprises the brief, seemingly insignificant relationships such as a little boy running into you on the street, someone whom you will never see again. The second level includes the intense relationships that are time circumscribed, having a beginning and an ending: childhood friends who do not see each other again; the therapist-patient or teacher-student relationship. The third level consists of lifelong relationships: families of origin, families that we establish later on, friendships we carry with us throughout our lives. The level of relationship makes no difference: if a little child runs into you and you do not judge the child, the ego is undone. The principle is quite simple: shared rather than separate interests.

> Even at the level of the most casual encounter, it is possible for two people to lose sight of separate interests, if only for a moment. That moment will be enough. Salvation has come (M-3.2:6-8).

Why do we pay less attention to the so-called trivial relationships and focus only on the major ones, when salvation could come the instant we do not judge a little child who bumps into our body, a big child who bumps into our ego, or a waitress who is having a bad day and forgets to bring the water? Why do we make a distinction? The purpose of the workbook lessons is to help us get past these spurious distinctions, because making them is the way we compromise with Jesus, saying to him that we will practice what he is saying here, but not there; we will apply his teachings in some situations, but not all situations. Beware of this tendency and do not judge yourself when you discover that you are compromising by asking Jesus' help to look at one kind of problem differently, but not another. Simply tell yourself that you are afraid of his love, and that these strange bargains with him are the defenses against it.

Underlying all the compromising is the awareness that there is a part of you that *wants* there to be problems, and that you do not want things to be healed. However, you do not want the situation to look like that, and therefore you work on healing some areas or relationships in your life but not others; you will practice part of the day but not consistently with all situations, all people, all the time. This, again, is the compromise we make with Jesus so that he will not be angry with us. It can look as if we are being holy, spiritual, and good *Course in Miracles* students because we are putting its principles into practice, but we must realize that deep down we do not want our problems solved.

One of Freud's major insights, as you recall, was that his patients did not really want to be healed or to get better. Anyone who does any kind of therapy— physical or psychological—knows there is a part of people that does not want to get better, which is why they so often don't. This is called resistance. This does not happen only in a therapist's or a doctor's office, but all the time. It happens with students of *A Course in Miracles*. As difficult as it is to accept this, we are comfortable with our problems; we like to feel unfairly treated, abused, victimized, and like a failure. And so we are not being honest when we claim we do not like ourselves because we are judgmental, angry, sick, and still indulging our specialness. We may think we do not like the way we are and wish we could be different, but the truth is that we *do* like the way we are, because if we did not we would not do any of these things. After all, it is our dream, our play. We are not only the hero and leading actor, we are the author. It is so very helpful to see this. Probably the most insidious of all special relationships is the one we have with our problems, our past abuse, victimization, and hurts—whether the past was this afternoon, yesterday, or sixty years ago. Once again, this is very hard to see, and yet it is important to look at this without judgment or guilt.

Another aspect of our fear of not being an ego is seen in the gospel story of Peter walking on water. He suddenly realizes what is happening, and then he sinks. "My God, look what I'm doing—I'm not an ego!" That is the fear we all feel when we truly forgive and let go of judgment. There might be a terribly difficult relationship, or a situation fraught with intense anxiety and fear, but we go about dealing with it differently from the way we did in the past. Then everything changes—not necessarily behaviorally—but certainly within. Then the terror almost inevitably comes. Its manifestation may be subtle, such as a sudden eating or drinking binge, sleeping for twenty-four hours, cracking up your car, or picking a fight with someone. It is the terror of not being an ego. Love is so intolerable to us, for the same reason God was so intolerable at the beginning. He did not throw us out of Heaven; we threw ourselves out, or believed we did. Since purpose is everything, we must have left Heaven for a reason, which is that love was intolerable. Why, identifying with the ego as we do, should it be any less intolerable now?

At some point, all of us who have worked with *A Course in Miracles* must have experienced a holy instant in which we actually let go of our egos; there was a clear sense that something was now different in a relationship or a situation. And then it is gone. That is when you get an irresistible urge to eat or sleep; you have an accident; you start fantasizing about some past hurt or future thing that you want—anything but staying in the present moment. When that occurs, it is helpful to be aware of what is happening. Even if you cannot stop yourself from going on a chocolate binge, or whatever, at least be aware that you are doing this because you became frightened of being quiet and peaceful, of living a few minutes without judgment or needs. The fear became overwhelming and so you had to distract yourself and make yourself sick. That is the same idea as in Lesson 136, to which I referred earlier:

> It is a choice you make, a plan you lay, when for an instant truth arises in your own deluded mind, and all your world appears to totter and prepare to fall. Now are you sick, that truth may go away and threaten your establishments no more (W-pI.136.7:3-4).

Truth arises in your mind and you become frightened. If truth is spirit, then you go back into your body and make yourself sick or indulge past addictions; you ruminate about the past and how unfair things are or how abused you have been. It does not matter. What is helpful is to see the causal connection between what you are feeling now—whatever the form—and the peace that you experienced beforehand. It might be that you read something in the Course and all of a sudden the lights go on; it becomes crystal clear that this is the truth, and this awareness cuts through your defenses. The next minute you find yourself at the refrigerator, on the telephone, turning on the television, becoming enraged at a news story, falling asleep, or simply forgetting totally what you just remembered. Everyone has had that experience, and it is very helpful to recognize that its cause is resistance. This is when you go back to dissociation and split off what you experienced as true. I oftentimes half-jokingly kid people who are attending my classes: "Watch what happens when you walk through those doors to the lobby. At the end of a session, everything you heard goes away. You are right back to carping, ridiculing, and judging someone, or making a beeline for the restaurant or the ice cream store or whatever." What is helpful is to see the causal connection between the experience of not being an ego, of not having judgment, anger, guilt, or anxiety, and the defense against that experience.

Your progress in *A Course in Miracles* can be measured not by diminishing ego attacks or chocolate binges, but by the shrinking of the reaction time between your being aware of what is happening and its happening. Even if you cannot stop the ego reaction, seeing the connection between the experience of love, of being in a non-ego state, and the defense against it, is what will speed you along. That is all you have to do. That is your progress. Do not force yourself not to binge, unless it is really going to hurt you (or others); do not force yourself not to engage in the defense. Rather, watch what you are doing and realize, "This just shows the height of my insanity. I felt so happy and peaceful, but now I feel overwhelmed with guilt because I am binging and know I am going to feel sick. Yet I am still choosing to do so because obviously I was terrified of being so happy and peaceful." That is all you have to do. Keep comparing the feelings of love and peace with the feelings of anxiety, tension, guilt, and sickness. The more you can compare them, and the closer you can bring the thoughts or feelings together, the closer you will be to ending the dissociation all together. It ends when you totally bring the illusion to the truth, or the darkness to the light. Robert Frost's poem "Mending Walls" comes to mind in this context. It begins: "Something there is that does not love a wall." That "something" is our right minds that feels suffocated by the absence of the loving light that would lead us home, and so it yearns for the forgiveness that undoes the wall, ends the dissociation, and restores our sanity.

Most people are used to working hard to change things such as self-defeating behavior so as to minimize the painful consequences. However, the general rule should be—and there are always exceptions to the rule or different ways of applying it—not to work at this. The ego is notorious and quite brilliant at setting up problems that are not problems, so that we become focused on trying to solve them. Remember though, *everything* here is a distraction! What you work at basically is not working at it, because the temptation is so strong to want to work at fixing the problem. We are a society that works at problems. We solve problems—that becomes our identity.

There is nothing wrong with doing things behaviorally. Obviously we have to solve problems behaviorally—for example, earning money so that we can survive, or learning how to stop self-defeating patterns that prevent us from functioning successfully in the world. However, the idea is to be able to solve the problem without thinking we are really solving the problem. This means, in a sense, that we know that "all the world's a stage" and our perceived problems are on the stage, and therefore they are make-believe. We thus go through our lives solving make-believe problems with make-believe solutions as if they were important (our *maladaptive solution to a nonexistent problem*), all the while sitting in the audience with Jesus enjoying the play. We know we are doing this right when we can enjoy the play, no longer seeing it as a tragedy but as a comedy. It is not so when we are on the stage, identifying with our physical lives in the world. The gentle laughter enters only when our identity has shifted and we are above the battle-ground with Jesus (T-23.IV), in our right minds, looking down on what we know to be a dream that has no effect upon the reality of God's Son.

Our lives were made to be very serious, individu-ally as well as societally. Societal problems ultimately are questions of life and death. It is very serious when people are in pain, physically or psychologically; it is very serious when huge groups in the world are in pain in different ways. That is the meaning of this line from "The 'Hero' of the Dream":

> It is not easy to perceive the jest when all around
> you do your eyes behold its heavy consequences,
> but without their trifling cause (T-27.VIII.8:4).

The "trifling cause" is separation or sin. "It is not easy to perceive the jest," in other words, to see the world or your personal life as a comedy, when all around you you behold the "heavy consequences" of life in a body. Millions of people are dying in Africa of AIDS and starvation; millions more around the world are suffering from bombs dropping on their heads, from cancer, from devastating earthquakes, tsunamis, and other "natural" disasters, from not having enough money to make their mortgage payments. Those are "heavy consequences," and Jesus is saying that "it is not easy to perceive the jest," to sit in the audience and see this as light-hearted fare when your eyes are looking at bodies dying, people acting in cruel, unthinkable ways toward each other, both individually and collectively. It is very hard to look at all that and realize it is a comedy, because your eyes are seeing only the "heavy consequences." We see the suffering body of a loved one, feeling its "heavy consequences," only because we do not recognize the "trifling cause," meaning we do not realize it is a dream. Again, this is the effect of having split off reality from appearances.

A Course in Miracles tells us that all this suffering is an illusion, and so it would be silly to give it power over our minds. That is why it uses words like *laughter* and *jest*. And so on the one hand we read these passages, understand them, study them, and believe them, striving to focus on what this course is teaching us. Yet, on the other hand, we have our everyday lives that are totally separate from these words: we have our daily trials and tribulations, "the thousand natural shocks that flesh is heir to," to quote Hamlet; we watch news programs about what is happening here and around the world, and it is all terrible. It is very hard to confront the world's events and smile. This certainly does not mean that we should be silly about it or laugh derisively, but we can learn to want to learn to greet each day with Jesus' gentle smile.

The difficulty comes because of the dissociative wall we have built between what the Course tells us is true and what our lives, senses, and brains tell us is true. We need to look at the fact that while we claim to be committed students of *A Course in Miracles*, we also close our eyes to what it says, finding ourselves suddenly becoming upset by things we know to be meaningless, or troubled by what we hear about the world or what is happening in our personal life at work, in our family, or in our own or a loved one's body. It cannot be said often enough that the mistake lies *not* in our becoming upset, but in rationalizing and justifying the upset by resorting to the world's laws and principles. Lesson 76, "I am under no laws but God's" should be understood at this stage in our learning as a way of helping us to remember that the body's laws work only because *we believe in them.* And so, as we follow their insane magic, we need only recall that this is simply part of a dream that we want to learn can have no effect on our minds.

A statement such as the one we just saw from "The 'Hero' of the Dream" becomes absolutely meaningless when we fail to recognize the "trifling cause." The next line says:

> Without the cause [the *tiny, mad idea* taken seriously] do its effects seem serious and sad indeed (T-27.VIII.8:5).

This is another way of Jesus telling us that what goes on in this world is certainly horrendous. The effects *are* very heavy. Much earlier he told us that "frightened people can be vicious" (T-3.I.4:2). Within the dream, the play that is our lives, millions die of disease and starvation when there are remedies and an abundance of food, but which are not provided to the people who need them; or when supplies for people affected by catastrophes do not reach them quickly enough. All this is serious indeed.

Yet it is difficult to look at these problems and situations without an accusing finger pointing at the very wrong people or governments that allow this to happen, or at the family, friends, or colleagues who are vicious and unkind. It is a challenge not to be angry or to feel hurt when there is so much suffering that could be easily averted or undone, when the Sonship of God appears to be fragmented into good and bad, the kind and the unkind, the haves and the have-nots. Nonetheless, the problem is not these dichotomies or the many forms of pain. The problem is simply that we forgot the "trifling cause":

> Without the cause do its effects seem serious and sad indeed. Yet they but follow. And it is their cause that follows nothing and is but a jest (T-27.VIII.8:5-7).

The effects are not the "jest." What makes it a comedy is not what occurs on the stage. What makes it a comedy is that it is a play masquerading as reality. When you actually see a play or movie, you know it is make-believe. When you get involved emotionally and psychologically, you have forgotten it is fiction; otherwise you would not care what you see. Becoming angry, anxious, sad, happy, exhilarated, or depressed when something happens on the stage or on the screen helps with understanding how dissociation works. Part of you knows that what you are seeing is made up—you are not psychotic; you know it is made up. In general, you know how films are made, how plays are written, cast, and staged; but, psychologically, that does not stop you from getting involved emotionally. That is dissociation, where one part of you does not tell the other part. This is exactly what happens with students of *A Course in Miracles*.

And so, one part of us knows how the world was made; that bodies are unreal; that "the world was made as an attack on God" (W-pII.3.2:1) because it came from a thought that was an attack on God—yet the thought never happened (M-2.2). Part of us knows all this, but that part does not inform the other part of us that is upset by what happens here, by what our or other bodies do, or by the news reports. It is the same as when we are sitting in the audience in a theater: the part of us that knows all of this is an illusion does not inform the other part. We can all identify completely with this phenomenon because it happens all the time, whether we are watching television, a movie, or a play. We know this is make-believe, but we also are aware of having emotions—positive or negative— that appear to be caused by this make-believe world we are looking at.

That helps us understand dissociation. Part of us knows the world is an illusion, that bodies are unreal, and we understand why bodies do what they do. Part of us understands, because we have read the sections that teach that attack is an expression of fear, and fear is a call for the love that has been denied (e.g., T-12.I.7-10). Yet that does not stop us from seeing attack and attacking in return: having an unkind thought, saying an unkind word, performing an unkind behavior. Nonetheless we understand that if we condemn one brother we are condemning ourselves and everyone else. We understand this because we have read it over and over again (e.g., W-pI.196,198).

If you are familiar with *A Course in Miracles*, you know how often Jesus uses the words *all* and *every*. We forgive *all* people; *every* brother has to be welcomed into the Circle of Atonement. *No exceptions.* That all-inclusiveness occurs throughout the entire Course. If you look for it, you will be astounded at how many times the words or the concepts *all* and *every* appear. You know that, but there is that wall, that dissociative split that allows you to forget the all-inclusiveness of the Course's message and proceed to attack or feel attacked, or judge someone as being less than you. Again, what will help you understand this dynamic is noticing what happens internally when you watch a movie, television, or the news.

It can also be helpful to compare waking and sleeping dreams in this context. While we are asleep and dreaming, everything in the dream appears to be real, but when we wake up and open our eyes, we realize that nothing that happened in the dream really happened. It is exactly the same in our waking dreams, but there is a split that prevents us from recognizing that fact. Thus, we maintain that there is a difference between our sleeping and waking dreams. The section, "The Basis of the Dream," specifically points out that our sleeping and waking dreams are the same:

> All your time is spent in dreaming. Your sleeping and your waking dreams have different forms, and that is all. Their content is the same (T-18.II.5:12-14).

Everyone who reads and studies *A Course in Miracles* knows this teaching, but when we open our eyes in the morning we live as if our sleeping and waking dreams are different. We think we are the innocent ones to whom things happen, and we forget that it is but our dream, even though we are repeatedly told that our very lives are a dream—*our* dream. Two other sections in the text are also very clear about this: "The Dreamer of the Dream" and the previously mentioned "The 'Hero' of the Dream" (T-27.VII, VIII).

Jesus' goal for us is that we become lucid dreamers, but not in terms of sleeping dreams. To be a lucid dreamer in the world's sense is to know that you are dreaming while still asleep. From the Course's point of view, however, the ultimate stage of lucid dreaming is the real world, where you are fully aware that life in the world is a dream, and therefore has no effect on you.

This course teaches that we could awaken in an instant. The problem is that we do not want to awaken in an instant, and that is why we have this dissociative wall. Following *A Course in Miracles* and practicing forgiveness day in and day out, letting go of our judgments and our special loves and hates (in attitude, not always in form), will awaken us from the dream. That is our goal. The fact that we hold on to our judgments of others and ourselves is telling us that we do not want the goal. If we did, we would employ the means that would lead us to it; but if we turn our backs on the means, it can only be because we do not want the goal. Thus we read in the text:

> A purpose is attained by means, and if you want
> a purpose you must be willing to want the means
> as well. How can one be sincere and say, "I want
> this above all else, and yet I do not want to learn
> the means to get it"? (T-20.VII.2:6-7)

To illustrate this point, let us say that I am going to
your home and I really do not want to go. I do not
know how to get there, but you have given me clear
directions. Then I get lost because I took a wrong turn.
One does not need a Ph.D. in psychology to understand that I got lost because I did not want to go to that
person's home. You gave me the means and I did the
exact opposite. I turned left even though your instruc-
tions said to turn right. You gave me the means to
obtain the goal that I did not want, and so I did not
attain it.

Jesus is quite clear that the goal of peace, awakening from the dream and returning home, is achieved
through the means of forgiveness. There is a lovely
prayer at the end of Lesson 189 that begins,

> *Father, we do not know the way to You*
> (W-pI.189.10:1).

We do not know the way, but God (meaning the Holy
Spirit) has given us forgiveness as the way. If we take
a wrong turn, meaning we judge instead of forgive, it

is because we do not want to reach the destination. We do not want to visit the person (i.e., our special love and hate partners) whom Jesus has instructed us to reach, for we do not want to reach God. That is why we split means off from End. It is extremely important to recognize that this is what is going on, and why we do not experience the peace that *A Course in Miracles* promises us will be ours.

We all awaken every morning with the same body we had the night before. The same figure is reflected in the mirror; we see and do the same things over and over again. It is not so important what we do with our bodies in terms of grooming, but it is important to notice that we do the same things with our bodies in terms of judging and holding on to grievances. What we need to do is be aware that we are judging, because we do not want to realize that everything that happens in our lives is an effect of a "trifling cause." We split off the cause, which again, is another form of dissociation. This is the ego's interpretation of the *tiny, mad idea*; and when we split it off, all we are left with is awareness of the effect. Then the effect without the cause seems very serious, "its heavy consequences." The world is clearly one gigantic "heavy consequence," and all the little "heavy con-sequences" are represented in our personal world.

It is not a sin to be afraid of this course, but it is a terrible mistake to pretend that you are *not* afraid of it. If you pretend that you are not fearful when you really are, you will have no means of undoing the fear. Within this world we are all creatures of our past, and it is terrifying to look at ourselves afresh, to be "born again" in the Course's sense of the word: without a past, which means without problems, his-tory, grievances, and so on. This is the content of the "Fear of Redemption" section (T-13.III), as I men-tioned earlier. We are afraid of the light, as we read in a later section:

> As the light comes nearer you will rush to darkness, shrinking from the truth, sometimes retreating to the lesser forms of fear, and some-times to stark terror (T-18.III.2:1).

St. Augustine, it appears, was the first to express this reaction. You go toward the light, and then all of a sudden it is as if you were slammed in the back of the head, finding yourself back in darkness. You get drunk on scotch or bourbon, or some other form of special addiction, or you become suddenly ravenously hungry, even though you ate just an hour ago. It is not your stomach craving food, the body's puny attempts at sustenance. It is your ego craving food as a defense against that experience of peace and being sustained by the Love of God (W-pI.50). The light is so terrifying that we pull a blanket over our heads and remain hidden in darkness. Yet, if we do not know we are doing this, we will continue this most maladaptive behavior. If we know we are doing it, at some point we will be able to make the contrast between the pain of living in the darkness of separation, specialness, and hate, and the peace that comes when we let our identification with the ego go.

I frequently quote this line from the beginning of the text:

> You have no idea of the tremendous release and deep peace that comes from meeting yourself and your brothers totally without judgment (T-3.VI.3:1).

This is a most important line, except it is not quite true, because there is a part of us that *does* know. It is because we *do* know that we run away from it. So judgment, the same as sickness, is a defense against the truth (W-pI.136). The icing on the cake is the "face of innocence": Yes, maybe I have judged you, but look what you did to deserve my attack! You cut me off on the freeway; you rejected me; you abused me. It does not matter whether it is a so-called major relationship in our lives or a trivial one. I have the right to be angry because of your sin. This is the final step in the ego's defensive system of protecting the fact that I am the one who judged you, who separated from God, who once again told the love of Jesus to get lost. I cling to judgment as the defense and then I project the blame onto you so that I am off the hook.

5. The End of Dissociation

Jesus gives us the solution to the problem of dissociation in the section in the text called "Sharing Perception with the Holy Spirit," beginning with paragraph 4, which contains the heart of the solution. Remember that to dissociate is to split off what we think we are afraid of. Ultimately, what we split off is love, in the presence of which our individual self disappears. We therefore split it off, and to ensure that we never heal the dissociation by bringing the two parts together so the light would dissolve the darkness, and therefore our special identities, we dissociate from our minds entirely and make a world. This world, as we have seen, is what Jesus teaches us to see as the vehicle for returning to the mind so that we can choose again. Similarly, by learning to integrate the Course's nondualistic metaphysical teachings with our everyday life, not giving power to the illusory world to take away our peace, we end our dissociation of *A Course in Miracles*, thereby allowing it to be the means to help us achieve the End.

5. The End of Dissociation

(T-14.VII.4:1) Our emphasis has been on bringing what is undesirable to the desirable; what you do not want to what you do.

This is the Course's emphasis: "bringing what is undesirable to the desirable." We bring illusion to truth, not truth to illusion. That is why we do not bring Jesus up on the stage with us, which is what the world has always done. That brings truth to illusion. It would be an attempt to correct the illusion, and if we correct the illusion, we have made it real. When we *look* at the illusion, however, which is the meaning of bringing the illusion to the truth, it dissolves. Thus, the miracle does not look on truth; it "looks on devastation" (W-pII.13.1:3); and when one looks on the devastation—bringing the devastation to the Holy Spirit—the darkness of hate disappears. How can the darkness exist in the presence of light? This of course is the ego's great fear, that its thought system of guilt and judgment would be gone forever when seen through the light-filled vision of forgiveness.

(T-14.VII.4:2-4) You will realize that salvation must come to you this way, if you consider what dissociation is. Dissociation is a distorted process of thinking whereby two systems of belief which cannot coexist are both maintained. If they are

brought together, their joint acceptance becomes impossible.

What we have dissociated is the memory of our Oneness as Christ, split off from awareness of our separate, individual identity. Separation and oneness cannot coexist, so we keep them apart. If we bring them together, "their joint acceptance becomes impossible." Guess which one will disappear? Thus, the fear is not of God's Love, but of what would happen to our illusory self in the presence of the truth.

No one is afraid of love. Since no one knows what love is, how can we be afraid of what we do not know, let alone understand? The separated self that is the ego, however, is aware that in love's presence, it can no longer exist; I, as a special individual, am gone. In this world, this means that in the presence of Jesus' love, our anger is gone. We do not lose this self right away. That does not happen until we reach the very top of the ladder, but we do lose a self that is angry, depressed, guilty, anxious, and sad, that feels neglected and unfairly treated. This is the self that dissolves. We still see the body every day in the mirror, but now it is smiling. We will not dread the thought of facing yet another day. In the end, the illusion brought to the truth dissolves the illusion entirely; yet in our experience within the dream, as long as we think we are here, what dissolves is the wrong-minded self of guilt and pain.

(T-14.VII.4:5) But if one is kept in darkness from the other, their separation seems to keep them both alive and equal in their reality.

The above is a clear description of dissociation. In making up its story, the ego says, "Yes, you are split off from love; but you had better be because love will destroy you." As we do not know what love is, we blindly take the ego's word for it. Similarly, as no one knows God, we believe the Bible's myths of special-ness, and relatively few have stepped back to question this insane portrayal of our Source. The Gnostics were one group that did question it, and in one wonderfully incisive passage they quote God's terrible traits as depicted in the Old Testament—His anger, jealousy, and homicidal, if not genocidal proclivities—and write: "What kind of God is this?" We all should ask, "What kind of God is this?" but do not, because it is our God, the God of our sinful, guilty, and fearful self. This is the One the ego says we should be split off from. We not only need to split off from Him in our minds, but because He will break through the mind's barriers, we need to make up a world to escape into collectively, and into the body individually.

This is why we cling so tenaciously to the body, and want our spirituality to involve the body and its world. If God or Jesus is involved in the body, it must be real. That is the best defense of all from the ego's point of view. Once we bring God into the illusion, He ceases to be God, and the illusion becomes divine, whereby people speak of the earth as divine, and our bodies as created by God. From the perspective of *A Course in Miracles*, all this is patent nonsense because it denies the reality of God and affirms our seeming reality as individuals. Dissociation preserves this insanity by dissociating the two thoughts, and then splitting off the mind from the body.

(T-14.VII.4:6-8) Their joining thus becomes the source of fear, for if they meet, acceptance must be withdrawn from one of them. You cannot have them both, for each denies the other. Apart, this fact is lost from sight, for each in a separate place can be endowed with firm belief.

We split off the ego from God or the Holy Spirit, and then believe the lies that are left. In other words, since we have forgotten what the Holy Spirit is—that there even is a Holy Spirit and a memory of who we are as God's Son—all we have is the ego thought system, which does become God's voice for us. It is a condition of *one or the other*. We can believe in either one separately, and do, but cannot maintain belief in them both simultaneously.

(T-14.VII.4:9-10) Bring them together, and the fact of their complete incompatibility is instantly apparent. One will go, because the other is seen in the same place.

This, again, is the ego's fear, and so we can understand why forgiveness is the key message of this course. It undoes the separation, the splitting off of two mutually incompatible thoughts. And in the world, we split ourselves off from each other all the time. We split off from individuals in terms of our neediness and specialness. We split off as groups—racial, religious, social, economic, national, and political. We are always keeping the Sonship split, which reflects keeping the right and wrong minds split off from each other. We are afraid that if we bring them together, our self will dissolve, because this self is kept in place by dissociating the illusion from the truth, preserving the belief that separation is real and oneness is a lie.

It can never be said often enough how essential it is to know that what happens in this world is occurring in the mind; what we do and think and feel as bodies are only symbols of the mind's dynamics we have been discussing.

(T-14.VII.5:1) Light cannot enter darkness when a mind believes in darkness, and will not let it go.

This is a very important statement. Light will not enter darkness if we do not want the light; and we do not want it because we believe the ego's lie, that God's light will destroy us. One of Jesus' challenges as our teacher, therefore, is to expose what the ego has taught us, and then to convince us it is a lie. It is all a lie because God would not think this way; He does not punish; He does not separate; He does not recognize what does not exist. God knows only Love, and as spirit we are part of that Love. That is all God knows. Everything else that we believe is made up. Yet if we do not believe and accept that it is made up, we will not be motivated to welcome the light. That is why the spirituality that is usually practiced in this world is merely specialness in different forms. It is the ego's spirituality, a God, a divinity that the world knows and can accept, because it makes the illusion of duality real. The world is terrified of, and will not accept, a

God that is not involved with this world. This noninvolvement reflects a nondualistic thought system that is more prevalent in the higher teachings of the East, but is more or less unheard of in Western spirituality, which is essentially biblical and thus dualistic.

(T-14.VII.5:2-5) Truth does not struggle against ignorance, and love does not attack fear. What needs no protection does not defend itself. Defense is of your making. God knows it not.

These also are very important statements. "Truth does not struggle against ignorance." It merely shines it away. When you fight against ignorance, you have made it real, which is why nothing ever works in the world. The most sincere utopians have failed because they struggled against what they believed to be wrong, which only solidified the problem and by so doing, made it real. Recall that the miracle "looks on devastation, and reminds the mind that what it sees is false" (W-pII.13.1:3). It does not change, fight, or struggle with the world. To cite the workbook's statement on forgiveness: The miracle "merely looks, and waits, and judges not" (W-pII.1.4:3).

Remember, too, that this course is not about behavior. You can get involved in as many movements and causes as you wish, but work on doing so without judgment and without hating the other side. That takes hard work. But if you do not do this work of forgiveness, you will become further trapped in duality, and then there is no hope for any meaningful change to occur. Again, all utopian visions have failed because they have not gone back to this original thought that there is nothing out there to change; yet there *is* something inside that has to be changed. If you want to change what is external, you but solidify the defense of dissociation.

What is wrong with this world is the world, not what goes on in the world. It is the belief in the world itself that is the problem. If you try to change or struggle against it, without first changing your mind, you become part of it. The ego blesses that dynamic. The ego loves utopian visionaries, because they seem so holy and spiritual, and therefore become part of the same web that ensures that meaningful change will never happen. Again, this does not mean that you should not get involved in things of the world. You are a citizen of the world, of a country, and you have a body. Do whatever motivates you, but try to do so without judging. If you do it with judgment, you are doing it by yourself. If you do it without judgment, you know the Holy Spirit is with you. That is the real challenge that confronts us.

Terrible things happen in this world, but *everything* is terrible in the world. Cruelty comes in many forms: some are blatant and you cannot miss them; others more subtle. But *everyone* is cruel here. It is a cruel thought to leave Heaven and believe you destroyed it to satisfy your own special needs. Some people mask this extremely well, while others are right up front with it. Yet it is not the world's cruelty you want to change, but the cruel *thought* that you have chosen in your mind. Otherwise, there is no hope.

We move now to paragraph 6, which is another of those places—among dozens and dozens in the Course—where Jesus lays out very clearly and specifically what we are supposed to do:

(T-14.VII.6:1) The Holy Spirit asks of you but this; bring to Him every secret you have locked away from Him.

This says it all. Bring to the Holy Spirit every secret you have locked away from Him. It is not necessary to do anything external, or to meditate long periods of time each day. But it *is* necessary to look within your mind—the mind searching the early workbook lessons talk about—and bring to Him all your darkest thoughts, your guilty thoughts, and all your thoughts of sin and fear. And:

(T-14.VII.6:2) Open every door to Him, and bid Him enter the darkness and lighten it away.

Earlier in the text, Jesus asks us to be very honest with ourselves and not to hide anything:

> Be very honest with yourself in this, for we must hide nothing from each other. If you will really try to do this, you have taken the first step toward preparing your mind for the Holy One to enter (T-4.III.8:2-3).

He is saying the same thing here. He is not saying we should not have these thoughts, but rather that we should not hide them: "Sit with me in the audience, and together we will look at these thoughts of yours on stage, all these dark, hateful, cruel, guilt-ridden thoughts. But do not hide them from me, because when you hide them, you make them real, and then they can never be undone. They can be undone only when you bring them into the light of my love *and not judge them*." It is the same point he makes in "Practicing the Holy Instant":

> The necessary condition for the holy instant does not require that you have no thoughts that

> are not pure. But it does require that you have
> none that you would keep (T-15.IV.9:1-2).

This means that the problem is *not* the impure thoughts of the ego, but that our guilt makes us take them so seriously that we need to hide them from ourselves and from our teacher of the right-minded correction.

(T-14.VII.6:3-4) At your request He enters gladly. He brings the light to darkness if you make the darkness open to Him.

This is the process. It hinges on our wanting help and thus asking for it. The Holy Spirit does not break down the doors of our minds. We make the darkness open to Him. Yet how, we might ask, can we know there are dark thoughts in the mind when we do not know that we even have a mind? The answer is simple: we simply watch ourselves with other people; we watch our judgments, attack thoughts, and special-ness needs. That is all, for that is what will help us realize that they are all darkness, even when they seem to be framed in holy light. If there is any separa-tion involved, we know that reflects the darkened thoughts of the ego. We need to watch, therefore, how we perceive and interact with others, for that is when we need to ask for help. The help comes through Jesus showing us that what we see outside is the projection of the dark thought that we chose inside. It was the fear of the light, knowing that our darkened self-concept disappears in it, that led us to choose the darkness.

So this is all we do. It is so incredibly simple, and would be incredibly easy were it not for our resistance. We need to see how we forget and then make our problems so very complicated. In other words, we need to watch for our resistance and bring that to Jesus.

(T-14.VII.6:5) But what you hide He cannot look upon.

That is why we hide the ego's thought system. If we bring it to Jesus and he looks on it with us, it would disappear, along with the self we have erected on its foundation of guilt and hate. One could not ask for clearer statements about how we end our dissociation of love and *A Course in Miracles*.

(T-14.VII.6:6) He sees for you, and unless you look with Him He cannot see.

In other words, Jesus cannot see for us unless we choose to see with him, which is, in essence, what he meant when he told us that he needs us as much as we need him (T-8.V.6:10). He does not need us on the ego level, certainly, but he does need us in the sense that he cannot help us unless we ask him to. This course could not, and did not come through until Helen and Bill agreed that there must be another way of relating, and that they wanted to find it. That was the invitation that opened the door for Jesus to enter their conflicted minds and heal them.

If you do not feel a loving, nonjudgmental presence in your mind—and it does not have to be of Jesus or God; any symbol would work—it is only because you are afraid of it. This does not make you bad or wicked. It means merely that you are afraid. That is helpful information, for you are saying: "Here I am studying and trying to live this course, and yet there is another part of me, which I am trying to exclude, that obviously is afraid of it. I am not feeling the peace and the love that Jesus says is there for me." The temptation, of course, just as it was Helen's, is to blame him or the Course, instead of recognizing that it is our minds that are choosing against the peace that is already there, merely awaiting our decision to join with it.

And so, Jesus is saying to us: "Bring to me all dark thoughts. You do not have to let them go. You do not have to do anything except look at them with me."

This is what it means to bring them to him and see through his eyes.

(T-14.VII.6:7-8) The vision of Christ is not for Him alone [the Holy Spirit]**, but for Him with you. Bring, therefore, all your dark and secret thoughts to Him, and look upon them with Him.**

Once again, this is forgiveness or the miracle. Simple. We do not have to light a candle, say mantras, or practice rituals. Jesus is telling us that all we need do is look at our illusions with him. It is the looking without judgment that defines the healing process. To repeat:

(T-14.VII.6:8-10) Bring, therefore, all your dark and secret thoughts to Him, and look upon them with Him. He holds the light, and you the darkness. They cannot coexist when both of You together look on them.

It is bringing our darkness to the Holy Spirit's light that ends dissociation. The ego, however, convinces us to have Him look at the problems *in the world* and fix them. We want Him to come up with a plan to fix things here, meaning in *our* world, because we are terrified of His looking with us at our *inner* world, because that is where the problem is found: the mind's decision for guilt. This exhortation is a repetition of what Jesus said earlier in the text:

> We are ready to look more closely at the ego's thought system because together we have the lamp that will dispel it…. The "dynamics" of the ego will be our lesson for a while, for we must look first at this to see beyond it, since you have made it real. We will undo this error quietly together, and then look beyond it to truth (T-11.V.1:3,5-6).

(T-14.VII.6:11) His judgment must prevail, and He will give it to you as you join your perception to His.

And this, of course, is our fear, that the Holy Spirit's judgment *will* prevail over ours. It is only when we recognize that this hurts us that we are able to meet our responsibility to bring our perception to His, our darkness to His light. Again, we do not have to let the ego go. We do not do anything except look at it, without fear or judgment. Remember that the ego told us that its thought system of sin, guilt, and fear is monstrous. Looked at with the ego, these concepts are terrible, especially when we realize that the sin is against God, and our guilt means that this horrendous sin against God is in the very fiber of our existence.

We are not speaking of something relatively trivial as stealing jelly beans from a candy store, but that we destroyed Heaven! Every time we take a breath, it is a reminder of our sin, because the need to breathe makes the body real. The terror that ensues from this belief is overwhelming: God is going to destroy us. Who wants to look at such a monstrous thought system?

Recall this quote from "The Fear to Look Within":

> Loudly the ego tells you not to look inward, for if you do your eyes will light on sin, and God will strike you blind (T-21.IV.2:3).

This is a euphemistic way of saying God will destroy us. Since this is what we all believe, we do not look within, but without. We make up a body that can only look without, outside the mind. Jesus, therefore, is teaching us to want to see what is outside as the "royal road" that will bring our attention back to the mind, where, by changing our prior decision for the ego, we can be healed.

(T-14.VII.7:1) Joining with Him in seeing is the way in which you learn to share with Him the interpretation of perception that leads to knowledge.

This expresses our going from wrong-minded perception to right-minded or true perception, after which perception itself disappears in a gentle blaze of glory and we are home in the realm of knowledge. As our resistance wanes, the journey to this glory will become increasingly joyful.

(T-14.VII.7:2-4) You cannot see alone. Sharing perception with Him Whom God has given you teaches you how to recognize what you see. It is the recognition that nothing you see means anything alone.

We recognize what we see because we realize that what we see outside is a projection of what is inside, and nothing we see "means anything alone," meaning anything that is seen apart from Jesus. This also means that everything here is unified in its potential for reflecting either truth or illusion. Restated, true perception or Christ's vision sees *everyone* in the world as either expressing love or calling for it (T-14.X.7:1)—no exceptions.

(T-14.VII.7:5-7) Seeing with Him will show you that all meaning, including yours, comes not from double vision [the ego's and Holy Spirit's thought systems], **but from the gentle fusing of everything**

into *one* meaning, *one* emotion and *one* purpose. God has one purpose which He shares with you. The single vision which the Holy Spirit offers you will bring this oneness to your mind with clarity and brightness so intense you could not wish, for all the world, not to accept what God would have you have.

Notice how many times the words "one" and "single" appear: "*one* meaning, *one* emotion and *one* purpose"; "one purpose," "single vision," and "oneness." That unity is the end of the ego's game, wherein we see everything and everyone as the same, serving the one purpose of helping us heal our minds. When the mind is healed, love will flow through, and we will think, say, or do whatever will be helpful. If we truly care about ending suffering in the world, we need to begin with ourselves. People suffer terribly here, but we cannot help them if we are suffering, too, and we all suffer as long as we believe we are separated individual selves.

Therefore, Jesus asks us to want his help to end *our* suffering. Again, the love that suffering hides will flow through us and embrace everyone in his single vision and purpose. Healing, then, is inevitable—for us and for the world. Indeed, true healing cannot come through any external happening or intervention. What happens externally is simply the after-effect of our changing the cause that is in our mind: the decision to believe in the reality of separation and guilt.

6. "True Perception – Knowledge"

We close this book with a portion of the section "True Perception – Knowledge" from the clarification of terms at the end of the manual. This is a lovely way of bringing to a close everything we have talked about, for it expresses how we are to undo dissociation, ending the ego's attempts to keep us separated from our minds, from the Holy Spirit, and from the Love of God. We begin with paragraph 6.

(C-4.6:1) This is the shift that true perception brings:

In the past I often talked about the three steps of forgiveness. This paragraph summarizes those steps that shift us from the ego's guilt and attack to the Holy Spirit's forgiveness. Here is the first:

(C-4.6:1) What was projected out is seen within...

This is what happens when we ask Jesus for help in a situation where we are upset, anxious, or fearful. His response is that what we are seeing outside is a projection of what is within. It is the role of the miracle, which establishes that we are the dreamer (mind) of the dream, not the dream figure (body), and that the content of the dream is not true (T-28.II.7:1). The second step follows naturally:

(C-4.6:1) …and there [in your mind] **forgiveness lets it disappear.**

In the first step, the guilt that we projected onto another's body and then attacked, is returned to the mind. The second step involves looking at the mind's guilt and affirming it is made up, too, just as the attack on another was solely our doing. Then the guilt can disappear, having been upheld only by our wanting it and believing it to be true.

(C-4.6:2) For there the altar to the Son is set, and there his Father is remembered.

The *altar* in *A Course in Miracles* almost always symbolizes the decision maker, the decision-making part of the mind that stands either at the altar that drips with the blood of the ego's guilt, or the altar that is strewn with the lilies of forgiveness.

This happy step occurs because we have decided to forget the ego and remember the Holy Spirit, thus undoing the dissociation. When we stand at the altar to the Holy Spirit in our minds, the ego is gone and the memory of God dawns on the healed mind. We have released our need for dissociation, and what we had chosen to forget now returns to awareness as the dream of separation softly dissolves into its own nothingness.

(C-4.6:3-6) Here are all illusions brought to truth and laid upon the altar. What is seen outside must lie beyond forgiveness, for it seems to be forever sinful. Where is hope while sin is seen as outside? What remedy can guilt expect?

We keep wanting to see the problems outside so that they will never be resolved, thereby preserving our individual and special self. The problem of sin can be resolved only when it is brought within, to the mind that conceived of it in the first place and gave it its seeming reality. But when seen truly for the illusion it is, sin cannot but evanesce, having been upheld solely by our belief in it. Returning our attention to the mind means re-evaluating its earlier decision, withdrawing belief in what has caused us pain and placing the power of our minds in the service of Jesus and his forgiveness.

(C-4.6:7-10) But seen within your mind, guilt and forgiveness for an instant lie together, side by side, upon one altar. There at last are sickness and its single remedy joined in one healing brightness.

God has come to claim His Own. Forgiveness is complete.

That is the third and final step in our healing. Dissociation ends as illusion is brought at last to truth's healing light. How can illusion remain in the presence of truth? What power on earth can withstand the Will of God and His Love? And so Jesus' comforting words close our book, as his love, which we have joined at last, is gently enfolded into the One Love that created us and that we are:

(C-4.7-8) And now God's *knowledge*, changeless, certain, pure and wholly understandable, enters its kingdom. Gone is perception, false and true alike. Gone is forgiveness, for its task is done. And gone are bodies in the blazing light upon the altar to the Son of God. God knows it is His Own, as it is his. And here They join, for here the face of Christ has shone away time's final instant, and now is the last perception of the world without a purpose and without a cause. For where God's memory has come at last there is no journey, no belief in sin, no walls, no bodies, and the grim appeal of guilt and death is there snuffed out forever.

O my brothers, if you only knew the peace that will envelop you and hold you safe and pure and

lovely in the Mind of God, you could but rush to
meet Him where His altar is. Hallowed your Name
and His, for they are joined here in this holy place.
Here He leans down to lift you up to Him, out of
illusions into holiness; out of the world and to
eternity; out of all fear and given back to love.

APPENDIX

Stranger on the Road

The dead are dead. They do not rise again.
And yet I see in You a look I knew
In One so recently destroyed and laid
Away to wither on a slab of stone.

I almost could believe – but I have seen
Your blue and bloodless hands and broken feet,
The way You crumpled when they took You down.
This is a stranger, and I know Him not.

The road is long. I will not lift my eyes,
For fear has gripped my heart, and fear I know –
The shield that keeps me safe from rising hope;
The friend that keeps You stranger still to me.

Why should You walk with me along the road,
An unknown whom I almost think I fear
Because You seem like someone in a dream
Of deathlessness, when death alone is real?

Do not disturb me now. I am content
With death, for grief is kinder now than hope.
While there was hope I suffered. Now I go
in certainty, for death has surely come.

Do not disturb the ending. What is done
Is done forever. Neither hope nor tears
Can touch finality. Do not arouse
The dead. Come, Stranger, let us say "Amen."

You said You would return, and I believed
Too long already. Now my eyes are sealed
Against the slender thread of hope that cuts
Into my calm despair. O let me go!

Your Word surrounds You like a golden light,
And I can scarcely see the road we walk
Because my eyes are veiled. Disturb me not,
I beg of You. I would not see You now.

Must I remember now? And yet the light
Seems even brighter, and the road becomes
A sudden splash of sunlight. Who are You
Who dares to enter into fear and death?

Your Voice reminds me of an ancient song
My lips begin to sing, although I hoped
It was forgotten. Now I hear again
A Word I thought had been forever dead,

As You had died. I cannot keep my eyes
From looking up. Perhaps I did not see
The things I thought. Perhaps this light has come
To heal my eyes and let them see again.

Lord, did You really keep Your lovely Word?
Was I mistaken? Did You rise again?
And was it I who failed, instead of You?
Are You returned to save me from the dead?

Dear Stranger, let me recognize Your face,
And all my doubts are answered. They are dead
If you are living. Let me see again,
And hope will be transformed to certainty.

The dead are dead, but they do rise again.
Let me remember only that. It was
The rest that was the dream. The light has come.
My eyes are opening to look on You.

(*The Gifts of God*, pp. 103-105)

THE SECRET WALL
("The Lighthouse" • Volume 15 Number 2 June 2004)

Kenneth Wapnick, Ph.D.

Introduction: The Place of Truth

There is a place in you where this whole world
has been forgotten; where no memory of sin and
of illusion lingers still. There is a place in you
which time has left, and echoes of eternity are
heard. There is a resting place so still no sound
except a hymn to Heaven rises up to gladden
God the Father and the Son. Where Both abide
are They remembered, Both. And where They
are is Heaven and is peace (T-29.V.1).

This is the real world, the place in our minds we
remain but an instant (T-11.VIII.1:5-7), before God
leans down and raises us unto Himself (T-11.VIII.
15:5). It is the place of truth within illusion:

In that place which you have hidden, you will
only to unite with the Father, in loving remem-
brance of Him.... But seek this place and you
will find it, for Love is in you and will lead you
there (T-13.III.8:3; 12:10).

This article explores how God's Love leads us to this hidden place, already present in our minds, by removing the ego's secret wall that bars the way to light, keeping the Son of God in darkness.

The Wall

The darkest of your hidden cornerstones holds your belief in guilt from your awareness. For in that dark and secret place is the realization that you have betrayed God's Son by condemning him to death.... For a darkened mind cannot live in the light, and it must seek a place of darkness where it can believe it is where it is not.... shrouded in guilt and in the dark denial of innocence (T-13.II.3:1-2; T-13.III.11:5; T-14. VIII.1:2).

This wall preserves the separated ego self we perceive as vulnerable and threatened. Almost all of us carry childhood, and even early-childhood memories of painfully distressing situations of being abused, humiliated, rejected, and—worst of all—unloved and uncared for. It is but a short hop, skip, and jump from these memories to the reductive conclusion that our adult feelings of anxiety and fear are traceable to these early years. Within the narrow parameters of our human experience, that certainly appears to be the case. However, even though we seem to be members of homo sapiens, we are really thoughts in the non-temporal, non-spatial split mind of sin or innocence, guilt or love. The innocent self has no walls that hinder love's free extension, but they are an inherent part of the self riddled with thoughts of sin and guilt, born of a self-concept of inferiority and evil. This is the self that has made its home in the world, surviving by walls of defense that keep the mind's hate-filled self hidden from awareness, and the world's projected selves of hate at bay.

Behind the wall is this self's only safety, for bodies were made to be vulnerable, living in a hostile, threatening world of other bodies. Thus we carved out and still guard a secret place that no one can touch. Indeed, that is how we muddled through childhood, adolescence, and adulthood, for we could not otherwise protect ourselves from the mistreatment of the more powerful figures and forces in the world. Our only hope for survival has been to insulate ourselves from such incursions on our safety, for nothing can hurt our minds. Thus you can be as abusive and hurtful as you wish, but within my secret walls, where I alone rule, I need never forgive you. You may make my body submit to torture and domination, have me say whatever you demand, but you cannot affect *my* thoughts within *my* kingdom. This fortress is impregnable and impenetrable, and my specialness sacrosanct, allowing no one, especially figures of love, to threaten my bastions of hate. Indeed, gentle and loving hands are not allowed, for the hate would dissolve at their touch and my little self exposed to abuse, rejection, and annihilation.

Thus we vow never to let go of the fortress, which we protect by our judgments. As we grow, we become increasingly ingenious in these attacks, inventing justifications for remaining within our fortresses of specialness. The fear of losing our personal identity is the fear of losing the walls that keep us safe and secure. Our attack thoughts—of ourselves (guilt) and others (judgments)—keep that wall intact. We are terrified of forgiveness even loosening a few bricks, for then all will crumble, leaving us vulnerable and helpless, "at the mercy of things beyond [us], forces [we] cannot control" (T-19.IV-D.7:4). We keep our guilty selves hidden behind special relationships, and as long as there is one person from whom we withhold forgiveness, we are safe, for it only takes one to secure our separated self. Our only means of survival, therefore, is to carve out a little niche that belongs only to us, in which no one is ever allowed, lest we be hurt again. There is not a person walking this earth who has not built such a wall, saying to one's enemies and friends alike, and ultimately to God: "Thou shalt not enter here."

Jesus tells us that "To learn this course requires willingness to question every value that you hold. Not one can be kept hidden and obscure but it will jeopardize your learning" (T-24.in.2:1-2). Our fundamental value is to be safe within the secret wall that protects our separated existence. All other values—political, educational, religious, social, personal—stem from this world behind the fortress, which we defend so fiercely that not only can no one get in, *we cannot get out*. Thus we exist, imprisoned in our prison, defenseless behind our defenses, consumed by hate as we hate. The lie, which we have never questioned, is that somehow we are safe behind the wall, unaffected by the hate perceived outside the barrier. The ego deceives us into believing that our bodies keep us safe, since they are the objects of the world's venom and destructiveness, but this insanity camouflages the core identity of the vulnerable self, racked with guilt over its sin.

To recap, we begin by fearing the love within and build a wall of protection. Projecting our fear, we look for people's mistakes, calling them sins, which justify erecting a wall of judgment between ourselves and them. Behind this wall we cower in fear, terrified to venture forth beyond its narrow confines. How, then, can we ever move beyond the wall to the place of love, hidden beyond the mind's place of hate, which itself is protected by the wall of special bodies?

Moving Beyond the Wall— Looking with the Holy Spirit

The Holy Spirit's function is entirely communication. He therefore must remove whatever interferes with communication in order to restore it. Therefore, keep no source of interference from His sight, for He will not attack your sentinels. But bring them to Him and let His gentleness teach you that, in the light, they are not fearful, and cannot serve to guard the dark doors behind which nothing at all is carefully concealed. We must open all doors and let the light come streaming through (T-14.VI.8:1-5).

At some point the bitter solitude of life behind the wall—our little kingdom of fear and hate—becomes unbearable, for how long can one withstand the painful company of guilt, loneliness, and despair? Its pain is still more excruciating and sterile:

> In your tiny kingdom you have so little!... Look at the desert—dry and unproductive, scorched and joyless—that makes up your little kingdom (T-18.VIII.8:4,6).

Our disgust with fear's darkness leads us at last to question its reality, and this is all the space required for the Holy Spirit's Love to enter.

When we begin the process of seeking help from the Holy Spirit, we are asked to question this dual identity of a vulnerable body and guilty mind, reflective of the ego's double shield of oblivion (W-pI.136.5:2). That is why the process of looking at the wall meets with such heavy resistance, and calls for persistent and dedicated effort. Time is needed to break the identification with our bodily self, and identify instead with the decision-making part of our minds that chose this self, along with its defense. This is why the process of looking at the ego is so crucial. If I look at my ego in action, this "I" cannot be the ego. However, if I judge, I know it is the ego observing itself, for looking with Jesus means doing so *non*-judgmentally, even looking at myself failing to look. Thus I slowly begin the process of detaching from my ego. Only the fear of losing its special self delays the process.

The road to Heaven lies through hell, which means looking at our walls and the self we seek to protect behind them. *You cannot let the ego go without looking at it.* The ego defends itself by saying, reminiscent of Medusa and her head of venomous snakes: "If you look at me, you will be destroyed." Thus, the process inevitably entails hearing the voice of doom: "If I look, something terrible will happen because I am such a terrible person." Guilt and terror have always existed side by side in the mind, well defended by the secret wall. However, as the wall crumbles, the sinful self's pain comes through, as we become aware of the ego's fear of dissolution. Jesus points to this place of fear, to which God's Love would lead us, if we allow our Teacher to take our hands:

> Yet God can bring you there, if you are willing to follow the Holy Spirit through seeming terror, trusting Him not to abandon you and leave you there.... You are severely tempted to abandon Him at the outside ring of fear, but He would lead you safely through and far beyond (T-18. IX.3:7,9).

Yet we hesitate, for leaving behind our "friends" of separation and judgment means leaving behind our self:

> And now you stand in terror before what you swore never to look upon. Your eyes look down, remembering your promise to your "friends." The "loveliness" of sin, the delicate appeal of guilt, the "holy" waxen image of death, and the fear of vengeance of the ego you swore in blood not to desert, all rise and bid you not to raise your eyes. For you realize that if you look on this and let the veil be lifted, *they* will be gone forever. All of your "friends," your "protectors" and your "home" will vanish. Nothing that you remember now will you remember (T-19.IV-D.6).

It is helpful to recognize the ego's attempts to thwart this process of healing our special relationships. As *A Course in Miracles* states of the ego's advice:

> Now the ego counsels thus; substitute for this another relationship to which your former goal was quite appropriate. You can escape from your distress only by getting rid of your brother (T-17.V.7:1-2).

The workbook adds: "Another can be found" (W-pI.170.8:7). All this needs to be done quickly, because the threat to the ego is immediately painful for all who have identified with its thought system. Who does not know this dynamic? No sooner do we end one painful relationship or situation than we find ourselves in another; sometimes even within the same day. The pain of losing the wall is intolerable.

Yet allowing oneself to feel the pain is beneficial, in the sense of being the way to reach the love behind it. Krishnamurti spoke of this process when he urged his students, "Stay with the pain," meaning that if they stayed with it, they would find it is ultimately a thought that defended against love, the end of thought. In other words, bodily pain is a defense against the thought of pain, which in turn defends against love.

That is why Jesus describes the process of the holy relationship as "disturbed, disjunctive and even quite distressing" (T-17.V.3:3), and four of the six stages in the development of trust are depicted as painful, difficult, conflicted, and unsettling (M-4.I.3-8). When he says to us that "This is the time for *faith*" (T-17.V.6:1), he does not point to a magical god or elder brother who will fix our world, but to the mind's forgiveness. In fact, he tells us it is important to see that the special relationship involves a lot of pain (T-16.V.1:1)—the pain of the hurt we have concealed behind our walls of denial and projection, and did not wish to see. You cannot change something unless you look at it, and the pathway to the secret place of love entails looking beyond the secret wall that hides the secret place of guilt. We cannot change the guilt we do not know about, which conceals the false belief we vaporized Heaven. Those are extraordinarily painful ideas—not in the abstract, not intellectually, but in our experience. Our very existence is predicated on the "fact" that we have not only done sinful things, but are sinful and guilty in the very fibers of our being.

The reason magical savior figures are so popular—in Christianity, it is Jesus—is that they do the work for us. The traditional Christian understanding of redemption is vicarious salvation: Jesus did it for me by his suffering and death. That is why we find this important line at the beginning of "The Fear of Redemption":

> You may wonder why it is so crucial that you look upon your hatred and realize its full extent. You may also think that it would be easy enough for the Holy Spirit to show it to you, and to dispel it without the need for you to raise it to awareness yourself (T-13.III.1:1-2).

Looking upon hatred is painful, for it is the source of sin, and we would much rather "turn it over" to the Holy Spirit so as not to look at it in ourselves. Jesus cannot take our hate from us because we refuse to let it go, and thus we need to overcome our resistance and bring it to him. This means looking at it, which is why it so often seems as if things get worse. They were always worse; we just were not aware of it. When we strip away the veil and look at the ego with Jesus, we realize how horrific we were in our self-estimation. As the workbook says: "You think you are the home of evil, darkness and sin" (W-pI.93.1:1). Yet the pain of looking causes us to project the guilt, that we see it in others and attack them, and never experience it ourselves.

To summarize, the wall is not experienced as painful until we begin to understand its purpose. There is an aching loneliness and sadness in all of us, for we believe we ran away from home. Leaving Heaven by choosing against the Love of God is the source of the hurt, which we sought to barricade behind the wall so as not to feel it. Projection comes to the rescue, as we blame others for our pain. Yet the protection it affords is not real, because what it protects is not real, since we left Heaven only in dreams: We remain "at home in God, dreaming of exile" (T-10.I.2:1). Moreover, projection is an illusion, because *ideas leave not their source*—what seems to leave the mind but stays there, though hidden from view. The guilt we project being illusory, the result of the projection must be illusory, too. Healing is inevitable when you recognize that you merely project an illusion of separation. This leaves you in a state where you take nothing seriously in the world, since you recognize its unreality. On a practical level, this means the world has no effect on you, for it has no power to take away God's peace. This does not mean you ignore or deny what happens to the body, only that you deny its power to destroy the love in your mind.

We thus begin with the experience that the world affects us, but come to learn its effect is on the body, which is not our identity. This thought is central, for that means we are minds. Only with this recognition can we be unaffected by the world, which affects us when we give it power to do so. This means the problem is not you, nor what people have done. Students of *A Course in Miracles* know well the early workbook lesson, "I am never upset for the reason I think" (W-pI.5). It is the basis of forgiveness; the reason I forgive you for what you have not done—you might have attacked me, but you have done nothing to my mind.

Therefore, looking means taking the darkness I projected outside—anger, judgment, specialness—and bringing it within. I learn it is my darkness that I hold tightly around my self, and cherish because it walls off the light of love so threatening to my self. Forgiving my projected spots of darkness, I allow the light in my mind to extend throughout the Sonship. I hear everyone's call for help, for I have sought and found the quiet place of love:

> In silence, close your eyes upon the world that does not understand forgiveness, and seek sanctuary in the quiet place where thoughts are changed and false beliefs laid by (W-pI. 126.10:1).

Hearing the Call of Fear

> The Thought of God surrounds your little kingdom, waiting at the barrier you built to come inside and shine upon the barren ground. See how life springs up everywhere! The desert becomes a garden, green and deep and quiet, offering rest to those who lost their way and wander in the dust. Give them a place of refuge, prepared by love for them where once a desert was.

And everyone you welcome will bring love with him from Heaven for you.... And under its beneficence your little garden will expand, and reach out to everyone who thirsts for living water, but has grown too weary to go on alone (T-18.VIII.9:1-5,8).

Everyone is a frightened child who wants to be loved, and "has grown too weary to go on alone." Everyone. Jesus depicts the universal condition of pain and alienation in this poignant passage from the workbook:

This world you seem to live in is not home to you. And somewhere in your mind you know that this is true. A memory of home keeps haunting you, as if there were a place that called you to return, although you do not recognize the voice, nor what it is the voice reminds you of. Yet still you feel an alien here, from somewhere all unknown. Nothing so definite that you could say with certainty you are an exile here. Just a persistent feeling, sometimes not more than a tiny throb, at other times hardly remembered, actively dismissed, but surely to return to mind again (W-pI.182.1).

If you could be aware that returning home to love is all that people desire—no matter what they say or do—you would see the hurt child within them, and could not but hold their yearning in loving comfort.

To see the fearful, lonely child means allowing yourself to see the pain behind people's attack. No matter how vicious and cruel the behavior, there is still suffering underneath. Indeed, people would not attack *unless* they were suffering. No matter how hateful the objects of your judgment, they would not behave, say, or think as they do unless they were filled with the torturous pain of a little child who believes love has been taken away, and is left all alone in the universe, without hope.

Hearing the pain of alienation in others, as does a loving, caring adult with a frightened child, you reassure them that everything is all right, in whatever way is appropriate. However, if you do not hear the child's plaintive call for love, seeing an evil monster instead of the innocent child, it is only because you do not want to hear it in yourself. One could say that the goal of *A Course in Miracles*, therefore, is to have us hear the pain behind the defensive wall in all people— victim and victimizer, you and I. Our hearts would then go out to everyone, touching them where they hurt, for healing is universally loving and kind. Walls are defenses, and without them love will enter.

Indeed, love is already there, and without our walls, it naturally extends to everyone.

This does not mean that on a societal level you condone people's errant or attacking behavior. We cannot, for example, leave people free to run red lights, let alone commit murder or rape. Yet, it is possible to prevent someone from acting in a homicidal, suicidal, or otherwise destructive way without punitive intent; restrictions and limitations can be imposed without anger or retribution. Interventions on the level of *form* may be the same whether one is angry or loving, but the *content* is quite different. The person knows on some level that the imposed limitation is necessary, but would hear the love or the anger behind the act, which is the true teacher. Since minds are joined, we respond only to the mind's content.

In our wrong minds, we seek but to protect the walls of specialness, judgment, and hate, for we insanely believe this protects us from love. Our fear demands the wall, forgetting we have erected it, aware only of the terrible things people have done to us. Thus we continue to project the wall—not the wall that keeps us from our Self (self from Self)—but the wall that keeps our self from the evil, sinful selves out there, for whom we are always on the lookout. How then could love be kind? How could it be one? How could it be true? In our right minds, however, if we see the hurt child, we lovingly reach through the wall and touch the pain. And it is gone. Healing the hurt of another can occur only because you did it for yourself. This is Jesus' vision of forgiveness: healing begins with your mind, and then extends through the walls of specialness to others. The wall is not broken through, but, in the wonderful phrase from the text, there is "a quiet melting in" (T-18.VI.14:6). You simply touch the pain in gentleness, and the ego's walls disappear.

That is why Jesus describes the Holy Spirit as not commanding, overcoming, or demanding; He merely reminds (T-5.II.7:1-8). His Love becomes our model, helping us not to demand from others, nor attempt to overcome or control them. We simply accept people where they are, knowing what they do in hate and fear does not ultimately matter, for love is there. Our only function, therefore, is to remind them gently of the truth that separation had no effect on love. *For love is there.*

I thus demonstrate that whatever your distress, it has no effect on my love, exemplifying the principle that whatever was done to you likewise has no effect on the love in you. Learning this lesson, then, is our focus, from the time we awaken in the morning to the time we go to bed at night. We learn by teaching, which means demonstration, for the only lesson to be learned and taught is that we are forgiven. In that holy instant the Sonship is healed, for we are one. That is why the concept of oneness is so crucial to accept, which happily occurs through recognizing that everyone is the same, reflecting Heaven's Oneness. This cannot be learned here, but we can be taught we *all* have a frightened child within, crying out in pain and hurt, wanting only to be held and taught that nothing happened to change love: "Regardless of what was done to you, or what you have done, you still are loved." Such forgiveness—reflecting Heaven's Love—is impossible as long as we hold on to the wall around ourselves.

We all, as one Son, suffer as one, our pain walled over to deaden it. We feel bad but do not know its source. The searing pain of aloneness is gone from awareness, protected by our defensive walls. However, through daily study and practice of *A Course in Miracles*, we begin to understand the ego and, looking at it, its walls begin to weaken and the hurt exposed. It is not that the pain was never there, but that the wall kept it from awareness. Revealed and brought to the light of forgiveness, the darkness of pain fades away. Experiencing this forgiveness, if only for an instant, makes withholding it ever more painful, motivating us to choose it again as quickly as we have chosen against it.

At the culmination of Jesus' final vision in the text, he says: "Not one spot of darkness still remains to hide the face of Christ from anyone" (T-31.VIII.12:5). All the ego requires is one darkened spot perceived in another, for that protects the spot of sin I believe is in me. When we exempt someone from our forgiveness, we exempt the same forgiveness in ourselves. If we see sin's blackness in another that can never be forgiven, it is because we do not want to see our inner light, but some dark cornerstone of guilt that we seek to keep by projection. We thus refuse to see the hurt child in others, attacking their innocence as we cannibalize every ounce of it for ourselves. And yet, if we allow ourselves to see the hurt and pain in others, our hearts would go out to them. As Jesus' love heals through us, extending to everyone, it heals us as well. And where are walls of hate when love has come?

Conclusion: The Three Steps of Forgiveness

You are not trapped in the world you see, because its cause can be changed. This change requires, first, that the cause be identified and then [second] let go, so that it can be replaced [third]. The first two steps in this process require your cooperation. The final one does not (W-pI.23.5:1-4).

We can summarize this article by reviewing the three-step process of forgiveness, which undoes the secret walls that prevent our remembering love's truth:

1) I recognize that the darkness is not in another, but in myself. This does not deny the darkened spots of sin in someone, but only that they are irrelevant to my perception. I understand that the darkness I made real in you by my reaction, originated in me, and thus I recall the projection and remove the wall I had placed between us. This is a painful step, for in the instant of recognition the pain of my guilt returns to awareness. I realize, in the image drawn from Lesson 190, that the gun pointed at me is not held by your hand, but my own. In other words, the guilt is not in you. *I* am the secret murderer.

2) I now understand, with Jesus' love beside me, that not only is it an illusion that you were the killer, the fact that I am a killer is an illusion, too. I made up the guilt in you because I made it up in me. Heaven's Love was only *believed* to be destroyed. In truth, not one note in its joyous song of oneness was lost

(T-26.V.5:4). Recognizing this happy fact completes my part in the Atonement, and the wall between my self and Self dissolves into nothingness.

3) We are taught that this step is not our responsibility. Once I look at the guilt I put in you and recall it, realizing it was only my dark fantasy, I have fulfilled my part. I looked at guilt without judgment, and remembered to laugh at the tiny, mad idea of separation, which allowed it to dissolve into the Holy Spirit's gentle laughter (T-27.VIII.6:2; 9:1). If I become afraid of love again, I need but let the tender hand of Jesus touch another's pain, and immediately his light of truth abolishes the darkness of illusion, as we together return to the place of truth we believed we had abandoned for the ego's home of separation and guilt. The secret walls of defense are no longer needed, and so have disappeared. In their place is the light of forgiveness, which shines the way to the home we never left. And thus it is no secret we are healed (T-27.VIII.13:9).

text

text (continued)

text (continued)

text (continued)

workbook for students

manual for teachers

clarification of terms

The Gifts of God

Foundation for A COURSE IN MIRACLES®

Kenneth Wapnick *received his Ph.D. in Clinical Psychology in 1968 from Adelphi University. He was a close friend and associate of Helen Schucman and William Thetford, the two people whose joining together was the immediate stimulus for the scribing of A COURSE IN MIRACLES. Kenneth has been involved with A COURSE IN MIRACLES since 1973, writing, teaching, and integrating its principles with his practice of psychotherapy. He is on the Executive Board of the Foundation for Inner Peace, publishers of A COURSE IN MIRACLES.*

In 1983, with his wife Gloria, he began the Foundation for A COURSE IN MIRACLES, and in 1984 this evolved into a Teaching and Healing Center in Crompond, New York, which was quickly outgrown. In 1988 they opened the Academy and Retreat Center in upstate New York. In 1995 they began the Institute for Teaching Inner Peace through A COURSE IN MIRACLES, an educational corporation chartered by the New York State Board of Regents. In 2001 the Foundation moved to Temecula, California. The Foundation publishes a quarterly newsletter, "The Lighthouse," which is available free of charge. The following is Kenneth and Gloria's vision of the Foundation.

In our early years of studying *A Course in Miracles,* as well as teaching and applying its principles in our respective professions of psychotherapy, and teaching and school administration, it seemed evident that this was not the simplest of thought systems to understand. This was so not only in the intellectual grasp of its teachings, but perhaps more importantly in the application of these teachings to our personal lives. Thus, it appeared to us from the beginning that the Course lent itself to teaching, parallel to the ongoing teachings of the Holy Spirit in the daily opportunities within our relationships, which are discussed in the early pages of the manual for teachers.

One day several years ago while Helen Schucman and I (Kenneth) were discussing these ideas, she shared a vision that she had had of a teaching center as a white temple with a gold cross atop it. Although it was clear that this image was symbolic, we understood it to be representative of what the teaching center was to be: a place where the person of Jesus and his message in *A Course in Miracles* would be manifest. We have sometimes seen an image of a lighthouse shining its light into the sea, calling to it those passers-by who sought it. For us, this light is the Course's teaching of forgiveness, which we would hope to share with those who are drawn to the Foundation's form of teaching and its vision of *A Course in Miracles.*

This vision entails the belief that Jesus gave the Course at this particular time in this particular form for several reasons. These include:

1) the necessity of healing the mind of its belief that attack is salvation; this is accomplished through forgiveness, the undoing of our belief in the reality of separation and guilt.

2) emphasizing the importance of Jesus and/or the Holy Spirit as our loving and gentle Teacher, and developing a personal relationship with this Teacher.

3) correcting the errors of Christianity, particularly where it has emphasized suffering, sacrifice, separation, and sacrament as being inherent in God's plan for salvation.

Our thinking has always been inspired by Plato (and his mentor Socrates), both the man and his teachings. Plato's Academy was a place where serious and thoughtful people came to study his philosophy in an atmosphere conducive to their learning, and then returned to their professions to implement what they were taught by the great philosopher. Thus, by integrating abstract philosophical ideals with experience, Plato's school seemed to be the perfect model for the teaching center that we directed for so many years.

We therefore see the Foundation's principal purpose as being to help students of *A Course in Miracles* deepen their understanding of its thought system, conceptually and experientially, so that they may be more effective instruments of Jesus' teaching in their own lives. Since teaching forgiveness without experiencing it is empty, one of the Foundation's specific goals is to help facilitate the process whereby people may be better able to know that their own sins are forgiven and that they are truly loved by God. Thus is the Holy Spirit able to extend His Love through them to others.

Foundation for A COURSE IN MIRACLES®

Temecula, California

Please see our Web site, www.facim.org, for a complete listing of publications and available translations. You may also write, or call our office for information:

Foundation for *A Course in Miracles*®
41397 Buecking Drive
Temecula, CA 92590
(951) 296-6261 • fax (951) 296-5455